OFFICIATING SOCCER

D1308943

A publication for the National Federation of State High School Associations Officials Education Program

Developed by the
American Sport Education Program

Human Kinetics

Library of Congress Cataloging-in-Publication Data

American Sport Education Program.
  Officiating soccer/ American Sport Education Program with National Federation of
State High School Associations.
     p. cm.
  Includes index.
  ISBN 0-7360-4761-1 (soft cover)
  1. Soccer--Officiating--Handbooks, manuals, etc. I. American Sport Education Program.
II. National Federation of State High School Associations.
  GV943.9.O45O44 2004
  796.334'3--dc22

                              20040005046

ISBN: 0-7360-4761-1

The Web addresses cited in this text were current as of July 2004, unless otherwise noted.

NFHS Officials Education Program Coordinator: Mary Struckhoff; **Project Consultant:** Tim Flannery, NFHS
Soccer Rules Editor; **Project Writer:** Thomas Hanlon; **Acquisitions Editors:** Renee Thomas Pyrtel and Greg
George; **Developmental Editor:** Laura Floch; **Assistant Editor:** Mandy Maiden; **Copyeditor:** Jacqueline Blakley;
Proofreader: Erin Cler; **Indexers:** Robert and Cynthia Swanson; **Graphic Designer:** Andrew Tietz; **Graphic
Artist:** Francine Hamerski; **Photo Manager:** Dan Wendt; **Cover Designer:** Jack W. Davis; **Photographer
(cover):** © Human Kinetics; **Photographers (interior):** Tom Roberts and Dan Wendt; photos on pages 22, 37,
39, 42, 43, 53, 54 (bottom), 55, 65, 66, 67, and 68 © Tom Roberts; photos on pages 94 and 107 © Photodisc; all
other photos © Human Kinetics; **Art Manager:** Kareema McLendon; **Illustrators:** Keith Blomberg and Mic
Greenberg; **Printer:** United Graphics

We thank the Champaign Park District in Champaign, Illinois, for assistance in providing the location for the
photo shoot for this book.

Copies of this book are available at special discounts for bulk purchase for sales promotions, premiums, fund-
raising, or educational use. Special editions or book excerpts can also be created to specifications. For details,
contact the Special Sales Manager at Human Kinetics.

Printed in the United States of America   10 9 8 7 6 5 4 3 2 1

Human Kinetics
Web site: www.HumanKinetics.com

United States: Human Kinetics
P.O. Box 5076
Champaign, IL 61825-5076
800-747-4457
e-mail: humank@hkusa.com

Canada: Human Kinetics
475 Devonshire Road Unit 100
Windsor, ON N8Y 2L5
800-465-7301 (in Canada only)
e-mail: orders@hkcanada.com

Europe: Human Kinetics
107 Bradford Road
Stanningley
Leeds LS28 6AT, United Kingdom
+44 (0) 113 255 5665
e-mail: hk@hkeurope.com

Australia: Human Kinetics
57A Price Avenue
Lower Mitcham, South Australia 5062
08 8277 1555
e-mail: liaw@hkaustralia.com

New Zealand: Human Kinetics
Division of Sports Distributors NZ Ltd.
P.O. Box 300 226 Albany
North Shore City
Auckland
0064 9 448 1207
e-mail: blairc@hknewz.com

OFFICIATING SOCCER

CONTENTS

PREFACE

It's no secret that officials are an essential part of sport. But how do soccer officials come to know their stuff? How do they keep all the rules straight throughout each game and season? Educational tools and reference materials are important for every official not only to learn this craft, but also to stay sharp. *Officiating Soccer* is a key resource for those who officiate soccer games at the high school level. The mechanics discussed here have been developed by the National Federation of State High School Associations (NFHS) and are used for high school soccer throughout the United States.

We expect you know at least a little about soccer, but maybe not much about officiating it. Or you might know lots about both. The overall objective of *Officiating Soccer* is to prepare you to officiate games, no matter what your level of experience. Specifically, this book will

- introduce you to the culture of officiating soccer,
- outline what is expected of you as a soccer official,
- explain and illustrate in detail the mechanics of officiating soccer,
- show a connection between the rules of soccer and the mechanics of officiating it, and
- serve as a reference for you throughout your officiating career.

Officiating Soccer covers soccer officiating basics, mechanics and specific play situations. In part I you'll read about who soccer officials are and which qualities mark a good official. Part I also differentiates high school officiating from youth, club and college levels and describes game responsibilities, including pregame and postgame duties. Part II, the meat of the book, describes mechanics and procedures for the dual system, diagonal system and double-dual system, all in careful detail. Part III highlights some key cases from the *NFHS Soccer Rules Book* and shows how you, the official, apply the rules in action.

Officiating Soccer is a practical how-to guide that is approved by the NFHS. This book is also the text for the *NFHS Officiating Soccer Methods* online course, which also has been developed and produced by the American Sport Education Program (ASEP) as part of the NFHS Officials Education Program. To find out how you can register for the online course, visit www.ASEP.com.

NFHS Officials Code of Ethics

Officials at an interscholastic athletic event are participants in the educational development of high school students. As such, they must exercise a high level of self-discipline, independence and responsibility. The purpose of this code of ethics is to establish guidelines for ethical standards of conduct for all interscholastic officials.

- Officials shall master both the rules of the game and the mechanics necessary to enforce the rules and shall exercise authority in an impartial, firm and controlled manner.

- Officials shall work with each other and their state associations in a constructive and cooperative manner.

- Officials shall uphold the honor and dignity of the profession in all interactions with student athletes, coaches, athletic directors, school administrators, colleagues and the public.

- Officials shall prepare themselves both physically and mentally, shall dress neatly and appropriately and shall comport themselves in a manner consistent with the high standards of the profession.

- Officials shall be punctual and professional in the fulfillment of all contractual obligations.

- Officials shall remain mindful that their conduct influences the respect that student athletes, coaches and the public hold for the profession.

- Officials shall, while enforcing the rules of play, remain aware of the inherent risk of injury that competition poses to student athletes. Where appropriate, they shall inform event management of conditions or situations that appear unreasonably hazardous.

- Officials shall take reasonable steps to educate themselves in the recognition of emergency conditions that might arise during the competition.

KEY TO DIAGRAMS

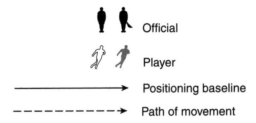

Official

Player

Positioning baseline

Path of movement

PART I

Soccer Officiating Basics

CHAPTER 1

INTRODUCTION TO SOCCER OFFICIATING

Perhaps you were one of the millions of kids who played soccer as a youngster (more than 7.7 million youth play soccer in the United States). You may have played at the high school, club or collegiate level. Maybe you enjoy the action, the strategies and the dedication that the game requires. You might see soccer officiating as a way to stay connected to a sport that you love and to stay in shape and have fun. Maybe you're a soccer official because you want to give back to the sport that has given you so much.

Whatever the reason, your involvement as an official is crucial to the life of the sport and the integrity of the game. Soccer has a great tradition throughout the world and is steadily growing in participation numbers in U.S. high schools, where more than 345,000 boys and over 300,000 girls play the sport. Soccer ranks fifth in terms of high school participation numbers for both boys and girls.

Just as it takes skill and training to be a great player, it takes skill and training to be a great official. This book will help lay the foundation for that training. The better you are as a soccer official, the better will be the games that you officiate.

Purpose and Philosophy

You have three main purposes as an official:

1. To ensure fair play by knowing and upholding the rules of the game

2. To minimize risks to players

3. To exercise authority in an impartial, firm and controlled manner as described in the NFHS Officials Code of Ethics (see page ix)

Ensuring Fair Play

Fair play is the foundation of all games. Nothing will get players, coaches or fans more irate than the belief that the rules are not being applied correctly and fairly. Competitors want and deserve an "equal playing field," so officials must know the rules thoroughly and apply them appropriately in all situations.

Two issues that often arise in high school soccer regarding an "equal playing field" are the *advantage rule* and the use of *international rules* rather than high school rules. When using the advantage rule, an official doesn't whistle a foul if the offended player retains the advantage. This call can be controversial because it is subjective—and of course coaches are biased toward their own players. It's very important to know the rule thoroughly and apply it consistently.

It is very common in soccer for officials to work games with different rules codes. It is not uncommon to officiate a club contest on Saturday morning and a high school contest on Saturday night. Some officials not only work club and high school but college contests as well. Officials who choose to do this must make sure they are familiar with the differences in the respective rules codes. Although the playing rules of the NFHS are similar to the National Collegiate Athletic Association (NCAA) and Fédération Internationale de Football Association (FIFA) rules, there are major differences in the rules for substitutions and misconduct. Additionally, the high school game uses signals to communicate to coaches, players and spectators.

The point is this: To ensure fair play, you must know the rules and enforce them the same way every time. When you do this, you go a long way toward being a good official.

Minimizing Risk

Like any sport, soccer has inherent risks of injury. Two players converge to head a ball. A defender attempts a sliding tackle in a tangle of legs. A midfielder dribbling the ball attempts a sharp cut on a wet or uneven field. And on and on—the chance for injury is part of the game.

As an official, your job is to minimize those chances and to respond appropriately when a player is injured. You can do this in the following four ways:

1. Know and enforce the rules. Many of the rules were written to minimize risks to players.

Playing by the Rules

Ed Halbrecht was a premier high school forward who went on to star in college. After college, Ed played on a top-level club team. He knows the sport inside and out and has been officiating at the collegiate level, the club level and now the high school level for many years. Ed is widely recognized as one of the top collegiate officials in his region.

So he's a great high school official, too, right? Wrong. Either because he hasn't taken the time to learn the high school rules or because he simply thinks high school athletes ought to play by a different set of rules, Ed makes many incorrect calls at the high school games in which he officiates. For example, he allows rethrows on throw-ins that do not get in bounds, he uses a drop ball to restart play even though a team was in control at stoppage, and he allows only one substitution on an injury.

Unfortunately, Ed's case is not an isolated one at the high school level. In fact, this is a pervasive problem. Part of the solution is better training and education for officials. Make sure you know and enforce the *high school* rules. Study your rules book until you know it backward and forward, attend rules clinics and keep up to date with rules changes. Confer with knowledgeable fellow officials about challenging situations that arise in games and ask them if they would have interpreted the rules and handled the situations differently. Give the players a chance to play by the rules they're governed by.

2. Inspect the field before the players take it and report any hazardous conditions to event management.

3. Maintain authority and control in all aspects, including interpersonal conflicts.

4. Know how to respond to injuries and emergency situations.

Exercising Authority

It's vital that you exercise authority in an impartial, firm and controlled manner. You can know the rules backward and forward, but if you can't exercise the proper authority you're going to have a difficult time as a referee.

Everyone involved in the game is looking to you to make the correct calls and to do so in a manner that doesn't call attention to yourself. Your mannerisms should let all concerned know that you not only know the rules but know how to apply them fairly and impartially, and that you have control over every situation.

Coaches and players go into most games respecting the officials and trusting in their ability to officiate fairly, but this respect and trust can be lost. You can lose respect and trust by making calls in an indecisive manner or appearing not to know the rules. Unfortunately, it is often difficult to regain this respect and trust once you lose it. And when you lose respect and trust, you lose control of the game.

Officials must be trusted by players and coaches in order to stay in control of the game.

To gain and maintain control of the game, know the rules, be firm and decisive and consistent in your calls, and make every call impartial. When you do this, you uphold the honor and dignity of the officiating profession. Coaches and players much prefer to have games called by referees who know how to maintain control, because then they know what to expect. Just as players are expected to prepare themselves to play at the top of their game, officials are expected to exercise control in calling the game. This doesn't mean you never blow a call; it means you never lose control of the game.

Who Are Soccer Officials?

Soccer officials come from all walks of life—bankers, insurance agents, business executives, factory workers, teachers, civil servants and so on. Some have played high school, college or club soccer; others' playing careers might have ended with youth soccer. Some are just out of high school; others are into retirement. Some may even be parents who never played soccer but fell in love with the game when their children began playing and use officiating as a way to stay in the game.

Despite these differences, good officials have much in common. They are critical thinkers who can make decisions in the heat of the moment while maintaining their calm and poise. They are able to act as peacekeepers and negotiators and know when to step into those roles. They know how to relate to coaches and players without demeaning themselves or harming the integrity of the game. They have thick skin and ample patience.

What Makes a Good Soccer Official?

Just as players need a mix of skills to be good players, officials need a range of skills to be good officials. And sometimes those skills can seem almost contradictory.

For example, to be a good referee, you have to blend into the background yet be omnipresent and authoritative. You must be an excellent communicator. You have to maintain control but keep the game in the players' hands. In the highly emotional arena of sports, you must keep your head while all others are losing theirs.

No one said being a good official is easy. But all good officials achieved their reputation by means of thorough preparation and dedication to their profession. You can join the ranks of good officials by following these eight prerequisites for good officiating:

Never Assume

If you want to be a good official, you should never assume anything. Always be prepared, concentrate on the game, anticipate plays and hustle. You are never

- so experienced that you've seen everything,
- so smart that you can't learn something,
- so good that you can't get better,
- so sure that you can't miss a call,
- so proud that you can't admit making a mistake,
- so right that you can't listen and talk to players and coaches,
- so superior that you can't mentor someone who wants your help,
- so worthy that someone else should not get the "big game" or
- so perfect that you shouldn't seek help when you need it.

Remember, if you're not working hard, growing and getting better, you are falling farther behind.

1. Stay in shape.

It is important to have an alert, healthy, sound mind, and it is equally important to keep your body agile and strong. Today's athletes are well conditioned, skilled and fast, and part of your job is to keep pace with them. Frequently, you'll need to move quickly to get into the best position to cover a play. If you aren't physically fit, you're a detriment to the game. Be in good physical shape before the season begins and be sure to get an annual medical exam. Maintain your good condition throughout the season.

2. Know the rules.

To be a competent referee you need to know the rules of the game thoroughly. Prepare yourself for making effective decisions through continual study of all possible situations and plays. If you are well rehearsed, fundamentals will become second nature and correct interpretations will be automatic.

To know the rules thoroughly requires constant analytical study and proper application of them. As you study the rules, form mental pictures of plays in your mind. These mental images will help you recognize the situations when they occur during games, and you'll be better prepared to make the right call. Remember, if your calls demonstrate that you don't know the rules, you will lose the confidence and respect of players, coaches and spectators.

3. Know the game.

Knowing the rules doesn't necessarily mean you know the game. When you understand offensive and defensive strategies, you'll be able to anticipate plays better, cover the field better and be in better position to make calls. The better you know the game from the player's perspective, the better off you'll be as a referee.

4. Know the mechanics and proper positioning.

Your knowledge of the rules and of the game might be outstanding, but if your mechanics are poor you will have a hard time getting your calls accepted. When a crew of officials uses proper mechanics, they are in the ideal positions to see all of the play clearly.

To be successful, officials, like players, must master the mechanics of the sport.

Several tools exist that will help you excel as a referee. The following list describes a few of them:

- *The current rules book.* Get it, learn it backward and forward, sleep with it under your pillow, know it as well as you can possibly know it.
- *Officiating resources.* Use this book and the *Officiating Soccer Mechanics CD (NFHS Edition)*, which shows animated mechanics, as well as magazines and other resources to help you hone your skills.
- *Firsthand experience.* Use every refereeing experience to learn, to improve and to expand your knowledge of the game and your ability to officiate.
- *Secondhand experience.* Learn from watching other good officials, either in person or on television. Observe their mechanics, how they comport themselves, how they exercise their authority, how they make their calls. Adapt what is useful to your own style.
- *Fellow officials.* Learn from their styles and discuss plays and other issues after games. Keep each other sharp in this manner.
- *Clinics and workshops.* Attend as many rules clinics as possible. If none are offered in your area, suggest to some veteran officials that local referees design one of their own. Speak with the schools in your area and develop a soccer officials' workshop. And don't stop with one clinic or course. Continue to learn throughout your career. Stay sharp; never get complacent with your learning.
- *A journal.* Use a journal as a self-assessment tool, charting areas for improvement, successes, progress and things learned from each game.
- *Review from others.* Ask a fellow referee from your local officials' chapter to watch you and critique your work if your state or local officials' association does not have a formal assessment program.
- *Self-review.* Have a friend videotape a game for your review.
- *Pre- and postgame meetings.* These are key learning times for referees, especially for beginners. If you're a new referee—or even if you're a veteran—there's no shame in asking more experienced officials for advice.

You need to master the mechanics, or play coverage, to be successful. It is important that you take the best position possible for any given play without being in the way of any player or the ball. Look for opportunities to discuss and review position and coverage at clinics and to practice the mechanics, whether you're a novice or a veteran. And remember that mechanics involves not only proper positioning but proper signaling, along with pregame and postgame procedures and responsibilities.

5. Know your style.

Every referee has his or her own style. Some go strictly by the book, but others allow for some gray areas in making calls. (We're not, of course, suggesting that you not adhere to the rules.) Some are serious disciplinarians, explaining no calls; others will take time to explain calls while maintaining authority. You aren't a robot in your day-to-day life, and you shouldn't be one on the field, either. An important aspect of being a good official is keeping consistency in your style and your calls. Know what your style is and be comfortable and consistent with it.

6. Be a good communicator.

Good communication is vital to good refereeing. That includes making verbal calls and making clear, correct signals. Give the proper emphasis to your calls. You don't have to be forceful on obvious calls, but on close calls make your call more forceful, using a strong, clear voice and clear signals. The way you signal not only communicates to players, coaches and fans, it may help sell the call.

7. Work in synch with fellow officials.

Good communication includes using body language and communicating—sometimes just through eye contact—with fellow referees. One use of eye contact is to get information from a fellow referee about a possible foul or misconduct. Talk through this issue with your fellow officials before the game begins so that you will be alert to this type of communication and when to look for it. As you gain experience, you will sharpen your communication skills in this area and will be working in synch with your fellow officials.

You should also have a mutual respect for your fellow officials. Friendliness and respect for members of the crew (and for the profession) contribute to confidence in one another. Try to support your partners throughout the entire contest. When a referee requests an opinion from you concerning a play, give it courteously only to the referee requesting it.

8. Be thick-skinned.

Know that you will be heckled by some fans and spectators. Every crowd includes fans who believe it's not only their right, but their duty, to insult the officials. Ignore insults, but not to the extent that crowd control becomes an issue. (That is, don't ignore your own duties to regulate crowd behavior.)

Those same fans who heckle you will lose respect for you if you react to their criticism or indicate that you're aware of their heckling. And when this happens, their criticism becomes more intense. Two traits of good officials are a deaf ear toward fans and a thick skin that is impervious to barbs and catcalls.

Officiating at the High School Level

Officiating soccer at the high school level is similar to officiating at other levels, but some elements can make the high school experience unique.

You might have refereed at youth levels where the officials sometimes "coach" the players during a game, giving them technique tips or allowing them to bend the rules as they learn the game. This does not happen at the high school level; you neither bend the rules nor coach the players. You simply call the game fairly and authoritatively.

With that said, the high school game can be seen in the larger context as a sort of "outdoor classroom," one in which players can learn some valuable life lessons—about handling winning and losing, about good sporting behavior, about full effort and teamwork, and about communicating with authority figures—in this case, with coaches and officials. Although you're there to call a game correctly and fairly, you will find moments when you can briefly explain to a player why you made a call—not to placate, but to educate. Sports at the high school level are really an extension of the classroom, and that makes you an educator as well as an official.

Systems of Play

Another difference among levels is the number of referees used. Some-times at youth levels you have only one referee; sometimes you have two. In high school soccer there are three systems of officiating: *dual*, *diagonal*, and *double-dual (three-whistle)*. It's generally up to the state association to choose which officiating system or systems will be used; if the association doesn't mandate the system, then the competing schools do so by mutual agreement. Following are overviews of the systems; for more complete coverage of these systems, see chapters 3 through 5.

Dual System

In the *dual system* there is a lead official and a trail official (see figure 1.1). One of these officials is determined to be the head referee while the second official becomes the assistant. Both officials have equal responsibility and authority in calling fouls, and the head referee makes decisions on any points not specifically covered in the rules.

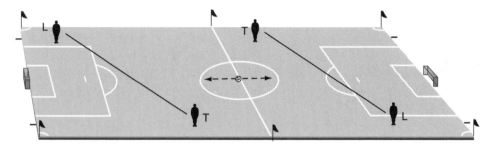

FIGURE 1.1   Basic officiating coverage in the dual system.

Advantages of the dual system include the following:

- Only two officials are needed.
- There are two different angles or sets of eyes on each play.
- Play is always boxed in by the two officials.
- There are two referees to communicate with players and to control violent conduct.
- Both referees gain experience in calling fouls that may help in retaining officials as being important to the game.

On the downside, the dual system sometimes results in referees being in poor offside coverage. If this occurs, the two officials might have conflicting views of a play. When the ball changes direction suddenly, the trail official becomes the lead official, which is the person responsible for judging offside.

Diagonal System

The *diagonal system* uses one referee and two assistant referees (see figure 1.2). The duties of the assistant referees (labeled AR1 and AR2 in figure 1.2) include indicating when the ball is out of play, when a player is offside and which team is entitled to the throw-in, goal kick or corner kick. They also assist the referee in controlling the game in accordance with the rules. The referee generally moves along a diagonal line from one corner of the field to the opposite corner (labeled A and B in figure 1.2). One assistant moves up and down one half of the field on one side; the other assistant moves up and down the other half of the field on the other side.

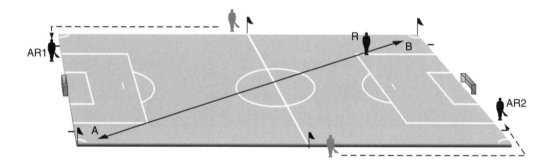

FIGURE 1.2   Basic officiating coverage in the diagonal system.

Advantages of the diagonal system include the following:

- One official makes the calls, leading to increased consistency.
- The system is used worldwide, so more training is available.
- Only one experienced official is needed.
- It allows for great offside coverage.

Challenges of the diagonal system include the following:

- Three officials are needed, as opposed to two.
- The referee, at times, may be at a poor angle, far from the ball.

- Assistant referees are permitted to indicate fouls and offside by signaling with their flag, but the referee must determine whether or not to agree with the call.

- Assistant referees have a lesser role than referees in the game. This is an excellent opportunity to recruit younger officials to work varsity games without the responsibility for making final decisions.

Double-Dual (Three-Whistle) System

The *double-dual* (or *three-whistle*) *system* uses a center referee and two side referees (see figure 1.3, a and b). The center referee (labeled CR in figure 1.3a) covers the center of the field, and the side referees (labeled SR1 and SR2 in figure 1.3b) cover most of the sides. The side referees have the same level of responsibility for game control as the center referee.

Advantages of the double-dual system include the following:

- Play on and off the ball is covered.

- It allows for great offside coverage.

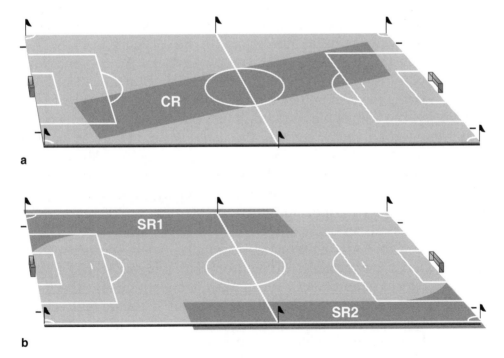

a

b

FIGURE 1.3   Basic officiating coverage for *(a)* the center referee and *(b)* side referees in the double-dual system.

- All plays can be covered by the center referee and one of the side referees.

- There are three officials to communicate with players, call fouls and to control violent conduct.

- Officials are promoted quickly to referee status.

- It gives all referees an integral part in the game.

- It minimizes dropout rate among officials because all referees are an integral part of the game.

On the downside, three officials are needed in this system which means that the total fees paid to referees may be more than other systems of officiating. As in the diagonal system, these officials are being paid. Also, foul calling may be inconsistent when the levels of officials are different.

That there are three systems of officiating, with differences in responsibilities and coverage, underscores the importance of fully understanding and preparing for the different systems of officiating. Responsibilities and coverage are explored in chapters 3 through 5 for these three systems.

There are rules differences as well—for example, at the high school level both teams can make substitutions on corner kicks; at the youth level (U.S. Youth Soccer Association rules) and at the collegiate level (NCAA rules) no substitutions can be made on corner kicks. At the youth and high school levels unlimited substitutions are allowed; at the college level players leaving the field in the first half cannot re-enter in that half, and players leaving the field in the second half can re-enter the game once. Regarding second yellow cards to the same player, in high school the player leaves the field and can be replaced; in college the player leaves the field and cannot be replaced. Throw-ins that do not enter the field of play are rethrown by the same team in youth play; in high school play the throw-in is given to the opposing team. Many other differences exist among the various levels.

In addition, the focus of the high school game—safety, sportsmanship, participation and education—differs from that at higher levels of play, where the focus is on player development, competition and spectator concerns. This is part of that "outdoor classroom" aspect of high school soccer; the sport is a learning tool for players, and the lessons learned on the field can be applied throughout a player's life.

As a high school soccer referee, you'll be part of the NFHS family which may include membership in the NFHS Officials Association, your respective state association or an affiliated local or district officials' association. Through these state and local associations you may receive assignments, publications and literature that explain rules changes and interpretations, you can attend annual rules meetings to learn new rules and hone your techniques and skills, and you can attend clinics throughout the year. Take advantage of these educational opportunities and continue to develop your skills and effectiveness as a high school soccer official.

CHAPTER 2

GAME PROCEDURES AND RESPONSIBILITIES

In chapter 1 we considered the main purposes of soccer officials, the qualities that make up a good official and the tools you can use to continue to develop your skills and grow in your profession. In this chapter we'll begin to get into the nitty-gritty of your responsibilities as a high school soccer official and the procedures to follow before, during and after games.

Pregame Procedures and Responsibilities

The head official is responsible for many of the pregame procedures, but the assistant officials share in those responsibilities and will assist the head official throughout the pregame preparation. The "Pregame Checklist" outlines, in chronological order, soccer officials' duties and responsibilities before a game begins. Unless otherwise noted, the responsibilities in the checklist are shared by all officials.

You should arrive in uniform at the field at least 15 to 30 minutes before the game is to begin. It's best to warm up as soon as you arrive at the field, because you'll be busy with other pregame duties shortly after you arrive. Give yourself ample time to jog and stretch (and make sure you're well hydrated, especially in warm weather) before the game.

Pregame Checklist

❏ *Hold a pregame conference with your fellow referees.* Review the duties of each official so that each one knows what they are responsible for before and during the game.

❏ *Meet with home institution officials.* The head referee should meet with the home school officials and inquire about any local ground rules. In terms of inclement weather or unsafe field conditions, up to game time it is the responsibility of the home institution to decide whether the game should be played. Once the game begins, it is the referee's decision as to whether it's safe to continue playing.

❏ *Check the field.* Conduct a pregame field inspection with the other referees. This is what you need to check:

• Field conditions. Is the field safe and playable? Will its conditions allow players a reasonable game experience? Among issues to consider here are whether the field is muddy, icy or has standing water; whether there are holes, uncovered grates, broken glass, rocks or dangerous ruts on or near the field; and whether it is raining hard, or it is foggy or lightning is nearby.

• Markings. Make sure field markings are correct, clear and distinguishable.

• Dimensions. Ensure that field dimensions are correct. This includes dimensions for the entire field and for the areas on the field (center circle, goal area, penalty area, corner arc and so on). For guidance on how to measure, see "Measuring Up" on page 26.

• Equipment. Check the goals, goalposts, crossbars, goal nets, goal post padding, corner flag posts and flags to make sure that they are in good working order and in accordance with the rules.

❏ *Meet with the coaches.* Meet with each coach individually, but don't linger in conversation or "shoot the breeze" with them. Likewise, don't discuss rules or calls from previous games. Simply introduce yourself and ask whether their players are wearing proper uniforms and equipment. Examine the uniform and equipment of each player to make sure they comply with the rules. If you go beyond this brief business with one coach, the other coach is likely to think that you might favor that coach in making close calls.

❏ *Observe players to get a feel for what to expect.* As the players warm up and prepare themselves for the game, assess their moves and abilities; you might pick up on some tendencies and skills that will help you anticipate plays and moves in the game—and thus help you get the proper angle.

❑ *Meet with the scorer and the timer.* Introduce yourself to the scorer and the timer, both of whom are designated by the home school. Go over their duties so they're clear on their responsibilities. Duties for the scorer include verifying each team's complete lineup, which should be submitted at least five minutes before the game is scheduled to begin, recording scores and keeping track of players who have been cautioned or disqualified. Substitutes also report to the scorer. Ask the scorer to hold substitutions until you signal for them to enter the game.

Duties for the timer include starting and stopping a visible timing device when signaled to do so by the referee, signaling to an official when a substitution is to be made and verbally counting down the final 10 seconds of each period of play so that the nearest official can hear it. The timer also signals when time has expired.

❑ *Verify that ball holders are in place and give them instructions.* The home team should provide at least two ball holders; they are under your direct supervision. They carry an extra game ball and retrieve balls that cross boundary lines.

❑ *Check the game balls.* While meeting with the scorer and timer, the head referee should check the balls that are to be used for the game. The home team should provide you at least three balls to inspect for game play. The balls should be 27 to 28 inches in circumference (#5 balls), made of weather-resistant leather or similar material, weigh 14 to 16 ounces and be inflated at 8 to 15 pounds per square inch. Squeeze the ball between the bottoms of your palms to check its firmness; if the ball is overinflated, let a little air out with an inflation needle (carry a needle with you). If the ball is underinflated, either have it inflated or test another ball.

❑ *Meet with the team captains.* Meet briefly with the team captains at least five minutes before the game is to start. Typically this meeting is held in the middle of the field, with the captains standing on their respective halves of the field. Flip a coin and have the visiting team captain call it while the coin is in the air. The winner of the toss can choose which goal to defend or to kick off. The loser of the toss gets the remaining choice.

❑ *Address coaches and players about good sportsmanship.* During the equipment check or the coin toss, the head referee should let the coaches and players of both teams know that they are expected to display good sporting behavior throughout the game. While most coaches and players know this is a general expectation of referees, when you state it, you leave no room for wondering whether it's important to you or not.

From *Officiating Soccer* by ASEP, 2005, Champaign, IL: Human Kinetics.

Game Procedures and Responsibilities

Here we'll give an overview of the general in-game responsibilities of all officials and of responsibilities specific to the head referee. We'll later build on that foundation by providing (in chapters 3 through 5) the mechanics of referees in the dual system, the diagonal system, and the double-dual system. We'll also address what to do at halftime and how to respond to injury situations.

Head and Assistant Official Responsibilities

Whether you are the head official or the assistant, these are your responsibilities throughout the game.

Stopping and Starting Play

Whistle play to stop, start or restart. Notify team captains when play is about to begin at the start of the game, following an intermission and after a time-out for injury. Stop or suspend the game for any infringements of the rules. Sound the whistle when the entire ball crosses a touchline or goal line unless it is obvious the ball is out of play.

On an advantage play, where calling a foul would actually hurt the team that was fouled, call out, "Play on!" and, with an underswing of both arms, indicate that you observed a foul but that you are not going to issue a penalty (see figure 2.1). If the advantage for the team that was fouled does not develop as you had anticipated, then immediately go ahead and call the foul.

FIGURE 2.1   Official calling play on.

Signaling

When you signal, be sure to use the official NFHS officiating soccer signals (see "Appendix" on pages 115-117). Signal the timekeeper when to start and stop the clock, and confirm for the scorekeeper the player to be credited with the goal.

When issuing yellow or red cards, hold the card with your arm fully extended above your head, indicate the player or coach cautioned (yellow card) or disqualified (red card) and notify both coaches, the scorer and other officials. It's helpful to use a reporting area when you make these notifications. The area should be about midway between the center circle and the officials' area, which extends about 10 yards on either side of midfield. If a player is being disqualified for a subsequent act of misconduct or taunting while receiving a yellow card, show the yellow card and the red card simultaneously in the same hand to indicate that the team can substitute for the disqualified player.

Working With Fellow Referees

Don't openly question another official's call when that call is made within his or her outlined duties. Don't override fellow officials' decisions (unless you are the head referee overruling an assistant referee). Discuss the matter in private with the official so that others (coaches, players and fans) don't know that you are discussing a call. This discussion could take place at halftime or after the game.

Good communication among officials is paramount for good officiating. That communication begins in the pregame conference, when responsibilities are discussed, and continues throughout the game.

Part of that good communication is using eye contact with fellow officials. Use times of slackened pace during the game to make eye contact with fellow officials to note the location of players and to make sure that all portions of the field are adequately covered. You can also use eye contact to confirm fouls or misconduct.

If you are the head referee, eye contact with assistant referees can assure good communication and teamwork among officials. Try to make eye contact with each official every time the ball goes out of play. It keeps everyone alert and in the game and reinforces the bond you should have with your fellow referees. And use eye contact to give affirmations: *good call, way to be in position, good judgment*. Watch also for assistant referees being harangued by a coach or a fan; if you see it, put a stop to it.

Head Official Responsibilities

In addition to the responsibilities just covered, if you are the head official you have these additional in-game responsibilities.

Ultimate Authority

In the diagonal system, it is your responsibility as head referee to confirm or overrule the assistant referee's signals. (In the other two systems, officials are equal for calling fouls.) There might be times when you have to overrule an assistant referee; do so without drawing undue attention to the assistant referee. Focus on correcting the call and keeping the game moving.

As head referee, you also have the power to make decisions on any point not specifically covered in the rules, such as equipment rulings and unusual situations.

Time and Score Issues

If the assistant officials disagree on whether a goal was scored, you will determine whether it counts. It is also your responsibility to keep time and score when no other means to do so is available. You will decide matters when the timer or the scorer disagree on timing or scoring issues. At the end of each half, check with the scorer and approve the score.

Termination of a Game

Once a game begins, it is in your jurisdiction. You have the power to terminate or suspend a game when conditions warrant. These conditions include unsafe field conditions, inclement weather, the behavior of those present or any other factor that would make it unsafe or unwise to continue play. If a game is terminated, complete a report and send it to the proper administrative authority.

Halftime

At halftime, regroup with the other referees, relax and talk over any issues that came up in the first half. Rest and rehydrate. A word to the wise: Don't leave your water bottles or gear near a team bench, because that gives a coach the chance to give you an earful.

It is game management's responsibility to alert teams that the second half is about to begin (this is normally done about three minutes before the end of halftime). Clarify with management that they will take care of this, then return to the field about two minutes before the second half is to begin.

Injuries

As cold as it might sound, when a player is injured and is being tended to, steer clear. It's not your responsibility to tend to injured players, and if you do you open yourself up to being named in a liability case. You also give the coach of the injured player the chance to accuse you of being the reason the injury occurred, because of the way you've called (or haven't called) the game. So move away from the injured player, but do monitor the coaches, because they aren't allowed to coach any player during an injury time-out.

When an injury occurs during a game, officials should steer clear while the player is being tended to.

For each game, you'll need to ensure that certain aspects of the field of play are in accordance with the rules. If markings are not made according to the *NFHS Soccer Rules Book*, ask the home maintenance crew to correct the markings prior to the start of the game. If the situation cannot be corrected, play the game and report the situation to the game authority. Safety issues such as improperly anchored goalposts, holes in the field of play, improperly installed nets or obstructions within 10 feet of the playing field must also be corrected before the game.

Following are recommended dimensions for a high school soccer field:

- Field of play: 100 to 120 yards long, 55 to 75 yards wide
- Boundary lines: 4 inches wide
- Halfway line marked across the field
- Center circle with a 10-yard radius drawn around it
- Goal area with lines at right angles to the goal line, 10 yards from the midpoint of the goal line, extending into the field of play for 6 yards
- Penalty area with lines at right angles to the goal line, 22 yards from the midpoint of the goal line, extending into the field of play for 18 yards
- Restraining line for penalty kicks, indicated by using the center of the penalty-kick line for drawing an arc with a 10-yard radius outside the penalty area
- Corner areas of the field, indicated by an arc with a radius of 1 yard from the intersection of the goal line and the touchline
- Goals, consisting of two upright posts, placed equidistant from the corner flags and 8 yards apart in their inside measurements. The crossbar of the goal is to be 8 feet from the ground.
- Goal posts may be padded with commercially manufactured material for soccer goals. This material shall be white, have a maximum thickness of 1 inch, be a minimum of 72 inches high and shall be properly secured.

You can ensure these dimensions in one of two ways—with tools or without. Over the years, officials become acutely aware when the goals are not the correct dimensions or the penalty mark is too close or too far from the goal line. Although it is a good idea to have a measuring device handy, it is not necessary to spend time ensuring that every measurement is 100 percent accurate. By knowing how long their stride is and determining distance by counting paces, officials can quickly check the more important distances, such as penalty mark, goal area, and penalty area.

To measure without tools, you need to know the length of your step, the height of your reach and your own height. To measure with tools, use either a measuring tape or a knotted string for key measurements. And remember to keep a pad and pencil with you to take notes.

Postgame Procedures and Responsibilities

After the game, verify the score with the scorer and exit quickly, leaving the field with the other referees. Just gather your gear and leave. As mentioned earlier, don't leave your gear by a team bench. A good alternative is to leave it beyond one of the goal lines. Game management should provide an escort to see you without incident to the locker room. Steer clear of team benches, coaches, players and fans; don't give anyone a chance to vent their frustrations to you.

Away from the field, report in writing any disqualifications and unusual incidents to the proper authorities.

After a game, talk with the other referees about the game's points of emphasis. Discuss critical plays and rulings and give feedback about each other's performance. Let the others know what they did well and things that they could have done better, and solicit that same information for yourself.

Later, evaluate your own performance. Did you apply the rules appropriately? Did you miss some calls? Was your coverage good? Did you maintain control of the game and protect the players? Did you communicate appropriately with coaches, players and fellow referees? What did you do well, and where do you want to improve? Were there altercations or incidents between opposing players, and if so how did you handle them? How did you handle rough or violent play?

Soccer is not an easy game to officiate. Don't be too hard on yourself, but do assess your performance and consider how to improve your abilities as an official. A great way to learn and improve is to ask a veteran official to observe you during a game. Then meet with that official afterward and discuss your performance.

Just as players aren't perfect, neither are officials. Be as prepared as possible for each game and use each game as a learning experience that you can build on. Go at it from a positive standpoint: Think about what you did well and consider how you can get even better.

PART II

SOCCER OFFICIATING MECHANICS

CHAPTER 3

DUAL SYSTEM

In the 1940s, the diagonal system of control (which is covered in chapter 4) was the only system for refereeing soccer. In the early 1950s, that system received competition from a new system: the dual system. This new system, composed of two referees, one designated as a head referee, was soon to become the popular system at both the high school and collegiate levels. It has been in use at these levels since the mid-1950s.

The dual system got its start in England, where matches using a head referee and a referee—as opposed to one referee and two linesmen—were played under the watchful eyes of Jimmy Walder and Harry Rodgers, who, together, conceived the dual system. It was well received in England, and Walder and Rodgers brought it to the United States, where college coaches were eager to try it out, in part because so often the referees in the diagonal system weren't trained. (Thus, it was not so much a downfall of the diagonal system as it was a lack of proper referee training programs that engendered the enthusiasm for the new system.)

And so a new system was born in the United States, not replacing the diagonal system, but becoming another choice for schools, clubs and organizations to consider (National Intercollegiate Soccer Officials Association, July 1997, *Interscholastic Division Newsletter*).

In this chapter we'll explore the dual system, discussing the general duties of each referee and the specific officiating mechanics to be used as they relate to

- movement patterns,
- calls,
- kickoffs,
- goal kicks,
- corner kicks,
- penalty kicks,

- free kicks,
- throw-ins and
- drop balls.

General Responsibilities

Before a game, you should meet with your fellow official to discuss your duties, establish a rapport and prepare yourselves for the contest. You should also use this time to discuss any difficult rules interpretations, points of emphasis or new rules.

Head Referee Responsibilities

The head referee should take care of the following responsibilities:

- Conduct the pregame conference and be responsible for the overall management of the game.
- Conduct the pregame meetings and instructions with the timer, scorer, coaches and team captains.
- Handle the coin toss.
- Inspect the field before the game and request that game management make any necessary corrections (see "Pregame Field Inspection").
- Speak with both teams and coaches before the game about good sporting conduct.
- Make decisions on any points not specifically covered in the rules.
- Be the final authority on any rules interpretations necessary during the game.
- Rule on legality of player equipment, paying particular attention to casts, bandages and padding protecting injuries.

Second Referee Responsibilities

The second referee has the following responsibilities:

- Take part in the pregame conference with the head referee.

- Assist the head referee in the pregame meetings with the timer, scorer, coaches and team captains; in the coin toss and in the overall management of the game. Address good sporting behavior with the coaches and players and ask coaches whether their players are legally equipped.

- Obtain team rosters before the game.

- Inspect the field with the head referee and call any irregularities to the attention of the head referee.

- Instruct the ball holders before the game begins. (The home team should identify at least two ball holders before the game.) They need to understand their responsibilities in keeping up with the play and in throwing the ball that they have before going after the ball just kicked out of bounds. Also, remind ball holders that they are part of the officiating crew and shouldn't be cheering for or against teams or players. Ball holders need to be alert and hustling throughout the game.

- Carry out other duties as directed by the head referee.

Pregame Field Inspection

When inspecting the field, you and the other official should walk the lines and inspect all areas adjacent to the lines. Also inspect each of the goals and nets. You want to ensure that

- the field is correctly lined;
- the goals are correctly placed and secured;
- nets are secured properly so that the ball cannot go through them;
- corner flags and halfway line flags are safely and properly placed;
- the field has no unsafe conditions, such as holes, raised sprinkler heads, uncovered drains or equipment placed too close to the playing area; and
- water is available on the field to drink.

Eliminate problem areas. Once the game begins, it is in your jurisdiction to determine whether field conditions are safe enough to continue play. Before the game begins, this decision is in the hands of the host institution.

Common Responsibilities

The head referee and the second referee have equal responsibility and authority in calling fouls (see figure 3.1, a-c). Don't question or set aside the decisions of the other official. When a call is in question, confer with your fellow referee to discuss the situation, far enough away from coaches and players that you can't be overheard.

a   b   c

FIGURE 3.1   Official calling a foul by *(a)* blowing the whistle, *(b)* indicating the direction and *(c)* indicating the type of foul.

The official on the side of the field where substitutions are entering should beckon the substitutes onto the field at the appropriate times. The official responsible for the restart will sound the whistle. See "Declaring the Ball Ready for Play" to learn which official is responsible for this declaration.

Declaring the Ball Ready for Play

Depending on the situation, either the lead or trail official is responsible for declaring the ball ready for play when a restart whistle is required.

The lead official ensures that all officials are ready for play and then declares the ball ready for play for corner kicks, penalty kicks and free kicks. The trail official ensures that all officials are ready for play and then declares the ball ready for play at the start of each half, for kickoffs after goals, for drop balls and for goal kicks.

For throw-ins, the official who is responsible for ruling on the legality of the throw must ensure that all officials are ready for play and then declare the ball ready for play.

Reserve Official

At times, a reserve official might be assigned to a tournament to assure game officiating continuity in case one of the assigned officials is unable to officiate. When a reserve official is assigned, the tournament authority will state the reserve official's role. The reserve official is under the jurisdiction of the head referee and performs those duties assigned by that referee. The reserve official's normal station, before being called into action, is at the table inside the officials' area during play.

Officiating Mechanics

As a soccer official, it's important that you know your responsibilities and your areas of coverage in all situations so that you are in good position to observe action and make necessary calls.

Throughout the rest of this chapter we'll cover the mechanics of the lead and trail officials in various game situations, beginning with their overall movement patterns.

Movement Patterns

How do you know whether you're in good position during a game? A simple rule of thumb is: At all times, you should be able to draw a diagonal line between you, the ball and your partner (see figure 3.2).

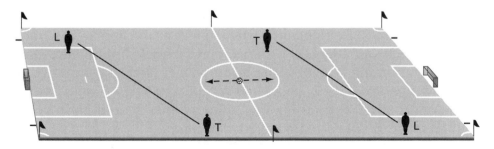

FIGURE 3.2   Officials' pattern of coverage in the dual system.

If you're the lead official, you'll normally be ahead of the ball on plays to either your right or your left; you can decide before the game, with your partner, which side you'll work to start the game (see figure 3.3). Change sides and directions for the second half.

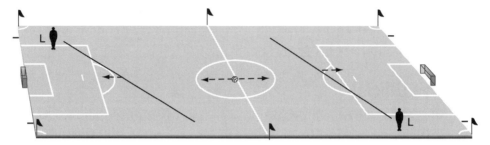

FIGURE 3.3   The lead official stays ahead of the ball on plays to the right.

In addition, you are responsible for covering the touchline and nearer goal line, and you must be in position to rule on offside. This means you must be in good position to know the position of the most advanced offensive player relative to the deepest two defenders at the same time the ball is played in the attacking half of the field (see figure 3.4). Once you observe the offside violation, make the call (see figure 3.5, a-d).

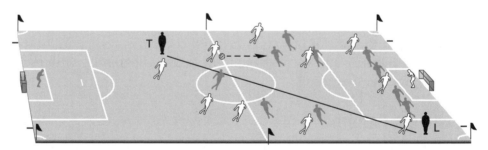

FIGURE 3.4   The lead official is in good position to observe an offside offense.

When you are the trail official, you will be behind the ball where the lead official will be ahead of the ball. Normally, in the first half, the official will lead to the right and switch in the second half to lead from the left. Direct your attention to play around the ball. Your penetration will depend on the type of game being played (kick-and-run or ball control—in a kick-and-run game you will penetrate less) and, to some extent, your physical conditioning, although you should be in good enough shape to always maintain good position.

FIGURE 3.5 Official calling *(a)* offside, *(b)* offside near, *(c)* offside middle and *(d)* offside far.

Sometimes it helps to penetrate 20 to 30 yards to help "box" the play (to see it from the best angle) and to preclude any guessing or missed calls from the touchline (see figure 3.6). A good example is when the attacking team is playing the ball in the far corner.

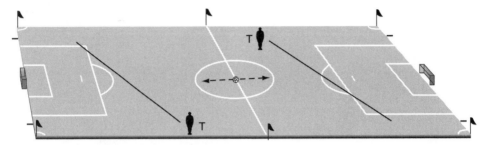

FIGURE 3.6   Proper field penetration by the trail official.

At times, the trail official will become the lead official and will rule on goal-line plays to the right. The position of the ball dictates which official will be responsible for off-the-ball coverage. For example, when the ball is near one official, the other official should be looking off the ball, such as in a breakaway.

Alert off-the-ball coverage is the hallmark of the dual system. If you were leading to your right in the first half, you would lead to your left in the second half. Because the teams change ends, you will have a different team in the second half than in the first.

Calls

An important part of your duties as an official is to make the right calls at the right time in the right way. When you observe a foul that needs to be penalized, you should follow these steps:

- Give a short, sharp blast of the whistle.

- Signal for time-out if appropriate. Call time-out for a penalty kick, caution or disqualification, after a score or when the head referee orders a time-out.

- Visually indicate the direction and type (direct or indirect) of free kick (see figure 3.7, a and b), the direction and spot of the throw-in, or the penalty mark where a penalty kick is to be taken.

a   b

FIGURE 3.7   Official signaling a *(a)* direct and *(b)* indirect free kick.

- Visually signal the foul.
- When required, if you are the lead official, you should give a sharp blast of the whistle, declaring the ball ready for play. Situations requiring a second whistle include restarting play for a penalty kick and after a substitution, caution, disqualification, injury or encroachment. You do not necessarily have to wait for the defense to set up to restart play.

Part of your role in making calls will involve issuing yellow and red cards (see "When to Issue a Card"). Here are the procedures for issuing a card:

- Sound the whistle and then stop the clock.

- Hold a yellow card or a red card—or both, if the situation warrants it—with your arm fully extended above your head (see figure 3.8).

- Do not extend your arm over the offending persons head.

- Indicate the player who is being cautioned or disqualified, recording his or her name and jersey number.

- Inform the scorekeeper, both coaches and your officiating partner the number of the player who is being cautioned or disqualified and the reason for the card.

FIGURE 3.8   Official issuing a card.

- Restart the game promptly.

Kickoffs

Kickoffs begin each period and are used to resume play after goals are scored. The positions of the lead official and trail official are shown in figure 3.9.

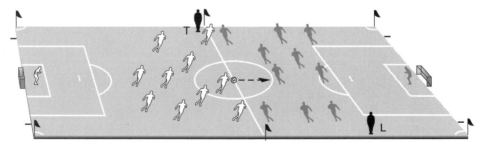

FIGURE 3.9   Positions of officials for a kickoff.

Some of the more common situations in which you would caution a player, coach or bench personnel by issuing a yellow card include the following:

- Unsporting conduct
- Incidental use of vulgar or profane language
- Objecting to officials' decisions either vocally or through body language
- Persistent infringement of the rules
- Entering or leaving the field of play (except through the normal course of play) without the permission of an official

There are also common situations in which you would disqualify a player. In the high school game, the number of players on the field is not reduced for certain disqualifications (yellow and red cards are simultaneously shown), while in others, the number of players on the field is reduced (red card only is shown).

Issue yellow and red cards—disqualifying the player, coach or bench personnel but not reducing the number of players on the field—for any of the following:

- Taunting
- Excessive celebration
- A subsequent caution

Issue a red card—disqualifying the player, coach or bench personnel and reducing the number of players on the field—for any of the following:

- Exhibiting violent conduct
- Committing serious foul play, including a player (other than the goalkeeper within the penalty area) who deliberately handles a ball to prevent it from going into the goal, or a foul by a player against an opponent moving toward his or her offensive goal with an obvious opportunity to score
- Using insulting, offensive or abusive language or gestures
- Leaving the team area to enter the field where a fight or altercation is taking place, unless summoned by an official
- Spitting at another person

FIGURE 3.10   Official signaling the ball is ready for play.

If you're the trail official, you should position yourself on the halfway line, near the touchline, with all players on the halfway line in front of you so that you can rule on any encroachment calls. If you're the lead official, position 10 to 20 yards from the halfway line and inside the touchline in the defensive team's half of the field.

If you're the lead official, check with both team captains, the scorer and the timer (if they are on your touchline) to obtain a "ready" sign from them before signaling for a kickoff. Additionally, if the timer and the scorer are on the trail official's touchline, that official should check to make sure they're ready. After you've obtained the ready signs, signal to the trail official that everything is set by extending your arm parallel to the ground, pointing in the direction the kick will be taken (see figure 3.10). The trail official will then sound the whistle to start the game.

Goal Kicks

When a goal-kick call is made, the trail official is responsible for declaring the ball ready for play for a goal kick. If you are the trail official, take a position near the top of the penalty area, approximately halfway between the touchline and the penalty area (see figure 3.11). You are responsible to see that the kick clears the penalty area before it is played a second time.

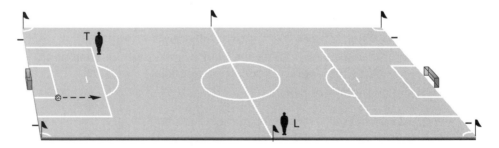

FIGURE 3.11   Positions of officials for a goal kick.

The lead official should be positioned near the field's halfway line and the touchline. As the lead official, you should determine your position by the kicker, the current wind conditions and how far you think the ball is likely to travel. Observe the players who are positioned in the area where the ball will be kicked, watching mainly for illegal pushing (see figure 3.12).

If the ball is kicked to the goalkeeper's right, perpendicular to the touchline, the lead official should see that the ball clears the penalty area before it is played a second time.

FIGURE 3.12   Official calling pushing.

Corner Kicks

The lead official is responsible for declaring the ball ready for play on all corner kicks if a second whistle is required. The positions of both officials are about the same, whether the kick is taken from the right side or the left side (see figures 3.13 and 3.14).

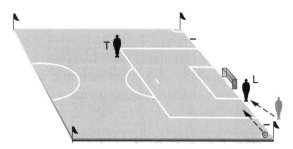

FIGURE 3.13   Positions of officials for a corner
kick from the right.

FIGURE 3.14   Positions of officials for a corner
kick from the left.

If you are the lead official, you are responsible for the flight of the ball
from the right or the left. Position yourself on the goal line between the
goalpost and the outer edge of the penalty area. After the ball is kicked
from the right, pivot to observe play while keeping track of the ball to
determine where it will land. As soon as you know the ball will land in
the field of play, forget the ball and direct your attention to the players
around where the ball will land.

If you are the trail official, position yourself near the top of the
penalty area on your side of the field, regardless of whether the kick
is taken from the right or left. On kicks taken from the right, observe
the goalkeeper and play around the goal area. Assume a position that
doesn't interfere with play but allows you to observe fouls in the goal
area.

When the kick is taken from the left side, the responsibilities are
slightly different. The trail official is responsible for placing the ball on
kicks taken from the left. When it is properly placed, the trail official
gives the second whistle if required. After the ball is kicked, the lead

official observes action on the goalkeeper and follows the flight of the ball to rule on the ball over the touchline. The trail official observes action in the penalty area, giving special attention to play in the goal area.

If a second whistle is required to begin play, the lead official should delay slightly before declaring the ball ready for play to give the trail official an opportunity to assume proper position.

Penalty Kicks

If you are the lead official, position yourself near the goalpost on your side of the field for a penalty kick (see figure 3.15). Hand the ball to the kicker and instruct the player to place the ball; then walk to the goalkeeper, making sure the goalkeeper is ready and understands that the ball will be released by the whistle.

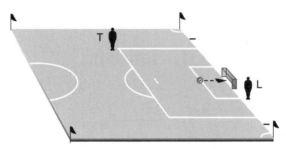

FIGURE 3.15   Positions of officials for a penalty kick.

When the goalkeeper and kicker are ready, declare the ball ready for play. Then act as goal judge and see that the goalkeeper stands on the goal line and does not move off the goal line before the ball has been kicked.

If you are the trail official, position yourself near the top corner of the penalty area opposite the lead official. Your responsibility is primarily to watch for infringements in the penalty area and penalty area arc by members of either team and for infractions by the kicker. As soon as a penalty kick is indicated, the official closer to the ball should pick up the ball and take it to the penalty mark. Both officials should assist the players in assuming positions for the kick.

Free Kicks

Positions for a free kick are shown in figure 3.16. When the ball has been properly placed for a free kick, the trail official indicates that the ball is ready for play by giving the appropriate free-kick signal (see "Appendix" beginning on page 115). Usually a player from the kicking team places the ball for a free kick.

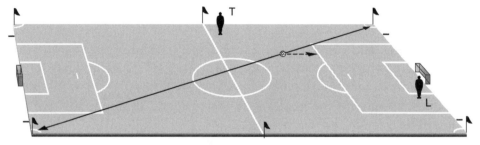

FIGURE 3.16   Positions of officials for a free kick.

FIGURE 3.17   Official calling holding.

Throw-Ins

If you are the official responsible for the touchline from which a throw-in is to be made, you will need to judge whether the throw-in is performed correctly.

If the attack is coming toward you, position yourself as the lead official and remember to anticipate how the play will develop. When the attack is away from you, your primary focus is to rule on the legality of the throw-in. The official on the opposite touchline should observe players in the general area around the throw-in, watching for holding (see figure 3.17), pushing and other fouls.

Drop Balls

For a drop ball situation, the two opposing players involved should position facing their goals. Other players can position themselves anywhere on the field, as long as they are not interfering with the drop ball action (see figure 3.18). Drop the ball from waist level between the players.

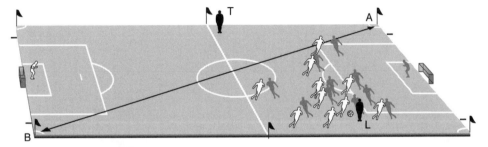

FIGURE 3.18   Positions of officials for a drop ball.

A game is restarted with a drop ball in the following situations:

- When the ball goes out of bounds and it cannot be determined which team caused it to go out

- When the ball goes out of bounds and a player from each team simultaneously causes the ball to go out

- When the ball becomes deflated or is losing air

- Following a temporary suspension of play and neither team has clear possession

- When simultaneous fouls of the same degree occur

The drop ball occurs in the spot on the field where the ball became dead unless it became dead in the penalty area. If the ball became dead in the penalty area, it will be dropped from the spot on the goal area line that is parallel to the goal line at the point where the ball originally went out of bounds. Additionally, the ball must touch the ground before either player can touch the ball.

Now that we've covered the mechanics for refereeing soccer in the dual system, let's turn our attention to the mechanics you'll need to know when refereeing in a different system of soccer: the diagonal system.

CHAPTER 4

DIAGONAL SYSTEM

The modern game of soccer arose from the game played in English "public" schools in the mid-19th century. Because the objective of these institutions was to train the future military and political leaders of the British Empire to behave as proper Victorian gentlemen, there was a strong motivation for players to follow the rules. In fact, the only game officials were umpires on the touchlines, one appointed by each team. Should a situation arise that could not be sorted out by the players themselves (an infrequent occurrence by most reports), the offended team's umpire would raise a handkerchief to stop play. The umpires conferred and determined the appropriate course of action.

As the game became more competitive, occasions arose in which the umpires could not agree, so a neutral third person, known as the referee, was appointed, to whom the team representatives referred their disagreement. By the early 1880s, the umpires had moved from the touchlines onto the field to be closer to active play, although the referee remained on the touchline and could intervene only if requested.

The rise of major amateur competitions and of professional soccer in the late 1880s inevitably led to more aggressive styles of play. To provide more direct game control, the roles of the referee and the umpires were essentially reversed. The referee was moved from the touchline to the center of the field and was given authority to directly intervene to control play. Furthermore, he was given a whistle to use for that purpose. The team-appointed umpires were replaced with neutral "linesmen" and were moved to the touchline. Their authority was restricted to assisting the referee, and they were given sticks (and eventually flags) to replace their handkerchiefs. Thus, by the time of the "Great Amendment" to the Laws of the Game in 1891, the diagonal system of control as we know it today was essentially established (Sir Stanley Rous C.B.E., and Donald Ford, 1974, *A History of the Laws of Association Football*; Zurich, Switzerland: Federation Internationale de Football Association).

Today, the diagonal officiating system employs a referee and two assistant referees. In this chapter we'll cover the general duties of each official and the mechanics of the diagonal system as we consider

- movement patterns,
- calls,
- kickoffs,
- goal kicks,
- corner kicks,
- penalty kicks,
- free kicks,
- throw-ins and
- drop balls.

General Responsibilities

The referee's duties before and during the game are about the same as they are for the head referee in the dual system. The referee should do all of the following:

- Conduct the pregame conference and be responsible for the overall management of the game.
- Clearly indicate in the pregame conference how each assistant referee can best help.
- Conduct the pregame meetings and instructions with the timer, scorer, coaches and team captains.
- Handle the coin toss.
- Inspect the field before the game and request that game management make any necessary corrections (see "Pregame Field Inspection" on page 33 in chapter 3).
- Speak with both teams and coaches before the game about good sporting conduct.
- Make decisions on any points not specifically covered in the rules.
- Be the final authority on any rules interpretations necessary during the game.
- Rule on legality of player equipment, paying particular attention to casts, bandages and padding.

The assistant referees are equipped with flags and normally remain outside the field of play. They indicate when the ball is out of play, which team has the throw-in and assist the referee in controlling the game.

At times, a reserve official might be assigned to a tournament to assure game officiating continuity in case one of the assigned officials is unable to officiate. When a reserve official is assigned, the tournament authority will clearly state the reserve official's role. The reserve official is under the jurisdiction of the referee and performs those duties assigned by that referee.

The reserve official often helps with substitutions, timing and scoring, communicating with coaches and players, maintaining proper team-area decorum and providing insight to the head referee as requested. The reserve official's normal station, before being called into action, is at the table inside the officials' area during play.

Officiating Mechanics

As you might imagine, mechanics differ in the dual system and the diagonal system. In the diagonal system, the referee has more ground to cover and more calls to make than does the head referee in the dual system (or the center referee in the double-dual system). Following are descriptions of the mechanics for the referee and the assistant referees in the diagonal system.

Movement Patterns

It's easy to see why this officiating system is called the *diagonal* system: Look at the pattern of coverage for the referee in figure 4.1,

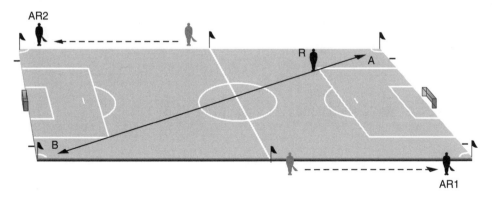

FIGURE 4.1   Pattern of coverage in the diagonal system.

from one corner of the field to the opposite corner. The diagonal line isn't a tightrope that the referee must stay on; it's a general guide for coverage and movement. As referee, you should be where the action is, placing yourself where you can get the best look and angle and bracketing play between yourself and your assistant referees. In a sense, the diagonal system can be regarded as a continuously varying and fluid dual system.

If you are an assistant referee (AR1 or AR2 in figure 4.1), you will move along only half of the field, from the halfway line to the goal line on one side of the field (see figure 4.2). As mentioned earlier, you will normally stay off the field as an assistant, going up and down the touch-line. You have the responsibility for the entire touchline and for the goal line toward which you are moving. (Note that the referee can choose to cover the opposite diagonal; in that case, the assistant referees would adjust as well. They always cover the half of the field that is farthest from the referee.)

As an assistant referee, you should stay even with the second-to-last defender on your half of the field or the ball, whichever is closer to the goal. For example, as the ball moves out toward the left touchline, the referee should move slightly off the diagonal to be near the play, and AR1 should move even with the second-to-last defender. AR2 should move into position for clearance of the ball and for a possible counter-attack, drawing even with the second-to-last defender on AR2's side of the field but never moving past the halfway line, even if the second-to-last defender moves into the attacking half of the field.

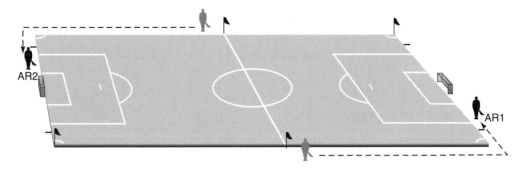

FIGURE 4.2   Assistant referees' coverage of the field.

Calls

If you are the center referee, make sure you fully use your assistant referees in calling fouls. The assistant referees have a different, and often better, view of the play and of fouls than does the center referee. Recognize and honor this by giving your assistant referees the power to call fouls.

When you observe a foul that needs to be penalized, and it is your call to make, you should follow these steps:

- Give a short, sharp blast of the whistle. If you are an assistant referee, hold your flag upright and wave it to get the attention of the head referee and then point it in the direction of the free kick when the head referee whistles play to stop.

- Visually indicate the direction and type (direct or indirect) of free kick (see figure 4.3, a and b), the direction and spot of the throw-in or the penalty mark where a penalty kick is to be taken.

a   b

FIGURE 4.3   Official signaling a *(a)* direct and *(b)* indirect free kick.

- Visually signal the foul (see figures 4.4 and 4.5 for an official calling a foul for kicking and tripping, or see "Appendix" on pages 115-117 for officials' signals).

- When required, give a sharp blast of the whistle, declaring the ball ready for play. You do not necessarily have to wait for the defense to set up to restart play.

FIGURE 4.4   Official calling kicking.

FIGURE 4.5   Official calling tripping.

As the referee, you will find it necessary at times to issue yellow and red cards (see "When to Issue a Card"). As an assistant, you can recommend that the referee issue a card, but you can't issue them yourself. Here are the procedures for issuing a card:

- Stop play and then stop the clock.

- Indicate the player who is being cautioned or disqualified, recording his or her name and jersey number.

- Hold a yellow card or a red card—or both, if the situation warrants it—with your arm fully extended above your head (see figure 4.6).

- Ensure that the offending player has left the field. Inform the scorekeeper, both coaches and your officiating partner why the player is being cautioned or disqualified.

- Restart the game promptly.

FIGURE 4.6   Official issuing a card.

Some of the more common situations in which you would caution a player, coach or bench personnel by issuing a yellow card include the following:

- Unsporting conduct
- Incidental use of vulgar or profane language
- Objecting to officials' decisions either vocally or through body language
- Persistent infringement of the rules
- Entering or leaving the field of play (except through the normal course of play) without the permission of an official

There are also common situations in which you would disqualify a player. In the high school game, the number of players on the field is not reduced for certain disqualifications (yellow and red cards are simultaneously shown), while in others, the number of players on the field is reduced (red card only is shown).

Issue yellow and red cards—disqualifying the player, coach or bench personnel, but not reducing the number of players on the field—for any of the following:

- Taunting
- Excessive celebration
- A subsequent caution

Issue a red card—disqualifying the player, coach or bench personnel and reducing the number of players on the field—for any of the following:

- Exhibiting violent conduct
- Committing serious foul play, including a player (other than the goalkeeper within the penalty area) who deliberately handles a ball to prevent it from going into the goal, or a foul by a player against an opponent moving toward his or her offensive goal with an obvious opportunity to score
- Using insulting, offensive or abusive language or gestures
- Leaving the team area to enter the field where a fight or altercation is taking place, unless summoned by an official
- Spitting at another person

Kickoffs

For kickoffs, the referee and assistant referees should be positioned as shown in figure 4.7. The referee should be ready to move up and down the diagonal and the assistant referees should also be prepared to move according to the play, staying even with the second-to-last defender in their half of the field or with the ball, whichever is closer to the goal line.

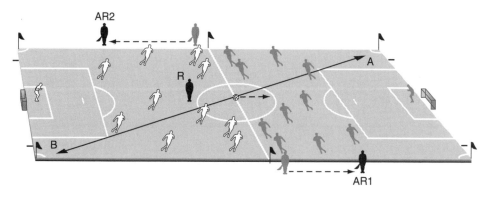

FIGURE 4.7   Positions of officials for a kickoff.

Goal Kicks

For goal kicks, the referee is near midfield (see figure 4.8). The assistant referee who is on the side of the field that the goal kick is taken should take a position in line with the outside edge of the penalty area after checking the ball placement (see AR2's position in figure 4.8). AR2 should make sure that the ball leaves the penalty area before being played a second time. AR1 assumes a position in line with the second-to-last defender and prepares for a possible attack by the team taking the goal kick.

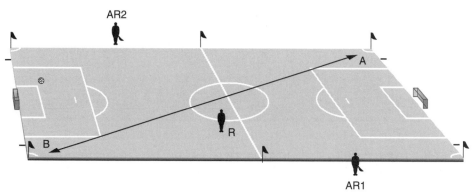

FIGURE 4.8   Positions of officials for a goal kick.

Corner Kicks

On a corner kick taken from the far corner, AR1 should move down the goal line to a position between the penalty area line closest to his or her touchline and the touchline itself (see figure 4.9). AR2 should move into position for clearance of the ball and a possible counterattack.

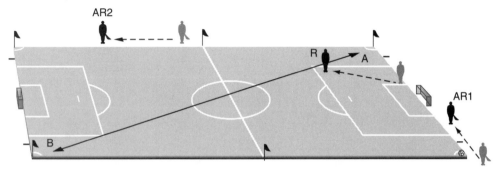

FIGURE 4.9   Positions of officials for a corner kick taken from the far corner.

On a corner kick taken from the near corner, AR1 should be in line with the goal line, a few yards behind the flag and the player taking the kick (see figure 4.10). AR1 should move down the goal line only if necessary to deal with encroachment. The referee should be positioned as shown in figure 4.10. AR2 again moves into position for clearance of the ball and a possible counterattack.

Regardless of where the corner kick is taken, AR1 observes whether the ball is properly played, makes sure that the ball is behind the goal line and opposing players are 10 yards from the ball, and watches for incidents that might be hidden from the referee.

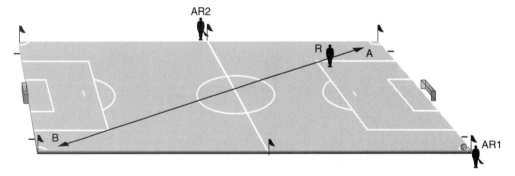

FIGURE 4.10   Positions of officials for a corner kick taken from the near corner.

On a corner kick in which the defense gains possession of the ball and begins a counterattack, the referee returns to position on the diagonal and the assistant referee on whose end of the field the corner kick was taken moves back to a position along the touchline, even with the second-to-last defender (see AR1's position in figure 4.11). The other assistant referee moves even with the second-to-last defender on the ball and gets in position to see any infringements and to indicate decisions until the referee regains position along the diagonal.

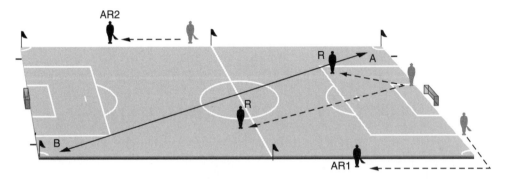

FIGURE 4.11   Positions of officials during a counterattack.

Penalty Kicks

On penalty kicks, the referee gets in position to see that the kick is properly taken, that encroachment doesn't occur and that the goalkeeper doesn't move forward before the kick. The assistant referee on whose side of the field the kick is taken moves in position to be able to ascertain whether the whole of the ball crosses the goal line (see AR1's position in figure 4.12). The other assistant referee is in position to cover play should the goalkeeper save the goal and begin a counterattack.

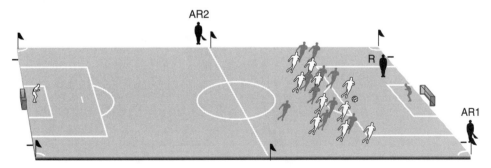

FIGURE 4.12   Positions of officials for a penalty kick.

Free Kicks

For a free kick near the halfway line, the referee should be positioned to properly observe play where the ball will land and the lead assistant referee lines up even with the second-to-last defender, in a position to judge whether offside or any fouls occurred (see AR1's position in figure 4.13). The other assistant referee is about halfway between the goal line and the halfway line, even with the second-to-last defender. This assistant makes sure that the kick is taken from the correct place and is ready for a possible counterattack.

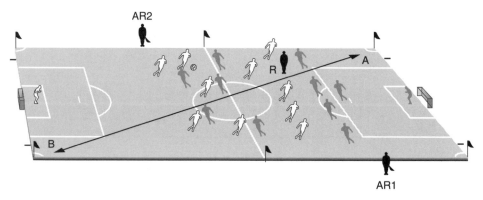

FIGURE 4.13   Positions of officials during a free kick near the halfway line.

For a free kick near the goal, the referee leads the play to observe wall behavior and will also act as a goal judge (see figure 4.14). When directed by the referee, the lead assistant referee on whose end of the field the free kick is being taken is near the goal line and will watch to see whether the whole ball crosses the goal line in a direct kick (see AR1's position in figure 4.14). The lead assistant referee should still be in position to watch

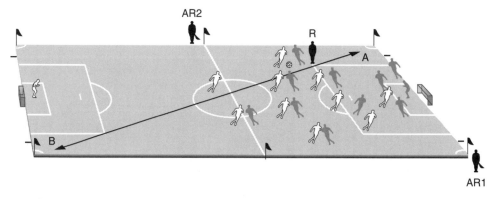

FIGURE 4.14   Positions of officials for a free kick near the goal.

for fouls and should also act as the offside judge. The other assistant referee should be even with the second-to-last defender in the defending half of the field or at the halfway line. Otherwise, the assistant referee will stay even with the next-to-last defender.

Throw-Ins

On throw-ins, the referee moves farther from the diagonal than on most other plays, going to the center of the field, or beyond, to get closer to the play (see figure 4.15). The reason for this position is that throw-ins do not normally go very far. In today's game, however, a throw-in can be just as long and powerful as a free kick, for example, from a flip throw. The referee needs to be able to judge where the play will result and position himself or herself to monitor the play. The assistant referee on whose end of the field the throw-in is taking place takes a position in line with the second-to-last defender. The other assistant referee does likewise on his or her end of the field and prepares for a possible counterattack.

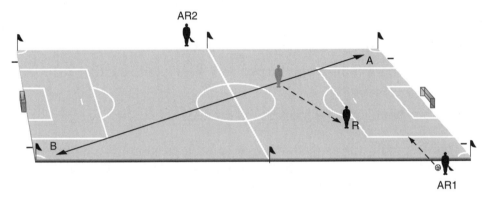

FIGURE 4.15   Positions of officials for a throw-in.

Drop Balls

For a drop ball situation, the two opposing players involved will face their respective goals. Other players can position themselves anywhere on the field, as long as they are not interfering with the drop ball action. The assistant referees should position themselves even with the next-to-last defender. The referee drops the ball from waist level when ready (see figure 4.16).

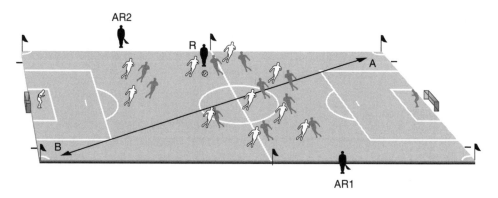

FIGURE 4.16   Positions of officials for a drop ball.

A game is restarted with a drop ball in any of the following situations:

- When the ball goes out of bounds and it cannot be determined which team caused it to go out
- When the ball goes out of bounds and a player from each team simultaneously causes the ball to go out
- When the ball becomes deflated or is losing air
- Following a temporary suspension of play and neither team has clear possession
- When simultaneous fouls of the same degree occur

The drop ball occurs at the spot on the field where the ball became dead unless it became dead in the penalty area. If the ball became dead in the penalty area, it will be dropped from the spot on the goal area line that is parallel to the goal line at a point where the ball originally went out of bounds. Additionally, the ball must touch the ground before either player can touch it.

Now that we've examined the mechanics of refereeing soccer in two systems—the dual system in the previous chapter and the diagonal system in this chapter—let's move on to the mechanics for another system that is used at the high school level: the three-whistle system.

CHAPTER 5

DOUBLE-DUAL (THREE-WHISTLE) SYSTEM

In 1965, a group of violent disturbances in Watts, a largely African American section of Los Angeles, resulted in the deaths of more than 30 people and the burning and looting of many businesses. It also is directly connected to the creation of the three-whistle, or double-dual, system of refereeing soccer.

Joe Bonchonsky was a soccer coach, a referee organizer and administrator in California when the Watts riots occurred. Bonchonsky was in charge of the soccer competition at the Watts Summer Games, and, because of the recent uprising, he was concerned about the problems that might occur on the field with only one head referee. He thought that referees needed more of a presence, so he gave the linesmen whistles instead of flags. And the Watts Summer Games soccer competition—with three referees—came off without a hitch (Harris, Paul, October 1993; *Interscholastic Division Newsletter*; Manhattan Beach, CA: National Intercollegiate Soccer Officials Association).

Thus, the double-dual system, using three referees (a center referee and two side referees) was born. In this chapter we'll explore the duties of each of the three referees and their mechanics in terms of

- movement patterns,
- kickoffs,
- goal kicks,
- corner kicks,
- penalty kicks,
- free kicks,
- throw-ins and
- drop balls.

General Responsibilities

The three referees share the officiating duties before and during the game. Together, they have the following responsibilities:

- Conduct a pregame conference with all referees to review individual responsibilities and overall management of the game.

- Go over responsibilities and duties with the scorer and timer before the game.

- Address all players and coaches about good sportsmanship. You may address each team together or separately.

- Handle the coin toss. Conduct a coin toss with the captains of the respective teams. The visiting team captain will call the coin while it is in the air, and the winner of the toss will choose a goal to defend or to kickoff. The loser of the toss will be given the remaining choice.

- Inspect the field before the game and request that game management make any necessary corrections (see "Pregame Field Inspection" on page 33 in chapter 3).

- Make decisions on any points not specifically covered in the rules.

- Act as the final authority on any rules interpretations necessary during the game. At times, there may be a disagreement among officials. In these rare instances, the center referee will determine the proper call or action.

- Rule on legality of player equipment, paying particular attention to jewelry, casts, bandages, padding protecting injuries, artificial limbs and other issues described in the *NFHS Soccer Rules Book*.

Making Calls

In the double-dual system, all three officials move on and off the field as needed. Their equal share in control means that a decision by any official is valid. To assure accuracy, all three officials should record incidents of misconduct. All are responsible for noting and penalizing violations of the rules. Officials should concentrate their attention in areas where patterns make their observation most effective. For example, while one official focuses on play around the ball, the other two focus on the action away from the ball while keeping the ball in their peripheral vision so that all players can be observed if possible.

The central duties of the center referee include observing and penalizing violations and boxing in play and players with the appropriate side referee—that is, "framing" the action so that the center referee and the side referee combine to have a complete view of the action. The center referee should evaluate situations in which the ball crosses the touchlines or the goal lines only if he or she has a better view of the play than the appropriate side referee or if the side referee requests assistance through eye contact. When disagreements between the center referee and side referee occur, the center referee will have the final word.

The side referees are responsible for boxing in play and players with the center referee, for determining offside violations and for calling fouls and violations. In addition, the side referees restart play after the ball has crossed either the touchlines or the goal lines.

When a goal is scored, the side referee nearest to the goal should quickly make eye contact with the center referee to confirm the goal and then signal for the clock to stop while indicating a goal has been scored by pointing to the center of the field (see figure 5.1, a and b). The center referee should confirm the goal by a quick nod, record who scored

a   b

FIGURE 5.1   Official calling goal.

the goal and then move into position for the ensuing kickoff. The side referees should also move into position for the kickoff. The side referee farthest from the goal should also record the goal, and the nearest referee should notify the scorekeeper regarding who scored. The side referee responsible for recording the goal may do so when time permits, such as halftime or at the end of the game.

On plays where it's necessary to signal that a goal has not been scored, do so as shown in figure 5.2, a and b.

a

b

FIGURE 5.2   Official calling no goal.

When you observe a foul that needs to be penalized, and it is your call to make, you should take the following steps:

- Give a short, sharp blast of the whistle.
- Signal for time-out if appropriate.

- Visually indicate the location, direction and type of free kick (direct or indirect), the direction and spot of the throw-in or the penalty mark where a penalty kick is to be taken (see figure 5.3, a and b).

- Physically signal the foul (see "Appendix" on pages 115-117).

- When required, give a sharp blast of the whistle, declaring the ball ready for play.

- Allow the attacking team the option to put the ball into play quickly, but if the attackers request a more formalized free kick, the referee may wait to restart play.

a   b

FIGURE 5.3   Official indicating (a) direct and (b) indirect free kick.

As a referee, you will find it necessary at times to issue yellow and red cards (see "When to Issue a Card"). Here are the procedures for issuing a card:

- Blow the whistle to stop play and then stop the clock by giving the clock stoppage signal.

- Hold the yellow card or red card—or both, if the situation warrants it—with your arm fully extended above your head (see figure 5.4). Each player or coach being carded must be shown the card separately. Keep other players and coaches away from those being issued a card.

- Indicate players who are being cautioned or disqualified, recording their names and jersey numbers.

- Inform the scorekeeper, both coaches and your officiating partner why the player is being cautioned or disqualified.

FIGURE 5.4   Official issuing a card.

- Allow substitutes to enter the game if appropriate.

- Restart the game promptly.

Restarting Play

The officials responsible for managing restarts and a second whistle when required are as follows:

Center Referee
- Start of play
- Offside

When to Issue a Card

Some of the more common situations in which you would caution a player, coach or bench personnel by issuing a yellow card include the following:

- Unsporting conduct
- Incidental use of vulgar or profane language
- Objecting to officials' decisions either vocally or through body language
- Persistent infringement of the rules
- Entering or leaving the field of play (except through the normal course of play) without the permission of an official

There are also common situations in which you would disqualify a player. In the high school game, the number of players on the field is not reduced for certain disqualifications (yellow and red cards are simultaneously shown), while in others, the number of players on the field is reduced (red card only is shown).

Issue yellow and red cards—disqualifying the player, coach or bench personnel but not reducing the number of players on the field—for any of the following:

- Taunting
- Excessive celebration
- A subsequent caution

Issue a red card—disqualifying the player, coach or bench personnel and reducing the number of players on the field—for any of the following:

- Exhibiting violent conduct
- Committing serious foul play, including a player (other than the goalkeeper within the penalty area) who deliberately handles a ball to prevent it from going into the goal, or a foul by a player against an opponent moving toward his or her offensive goal with an obvious opportunity to score
- Using insulting, offensive or abusive language or gestures
- Leaving the team area to enter the field where a fight or altercation is taking place, unless summoned by an official
- Spitting at another person

- Goal kicks

- Penalty kicks

- Drop balls

- Free kicks deep within the attacking end

- Substitutions (if center referee is closest to the ball)

- Corner kick (far corner)

Side Referee
- Free kicks (The center referee should take responsibility for free kicks deep in the attacking end, allowing him or her to observe play in the area where the ball is going to land.)

- Substitutions (if side referee is closest to the ball)

- Corner kicks (near corner)

- Throw-ins

- In situations requiring a second whistle, the side referee should control the restart if in the best position to do so

Regarding substitutions, the side referee nearest the bench should signal for stoppage of play at the appropriate time, allow the substitute to enter and signal for play to restart when the substitution is completed. This referee should make eye contact with the other officials before whistling the start of play.

Officiating Mechanics

Just as there are significant differences in officiating mechanics between the dual system and the diagonal system, the double-dual system presents a unique way to officiate soccer—and with its uniqueness come more distinct differences in its mechanics. Following are the mechanics for the officials in the double-dual system.

Movement Patterns

One of the most important distinctions of the double-dual system is in the movement patterns of the three referees, who all are on the field, as opposed to the two assistant referees who operate along the touchlines in the diagonal system. The pattern of coverage for the three referees are shown in figure 5.5, a and b.

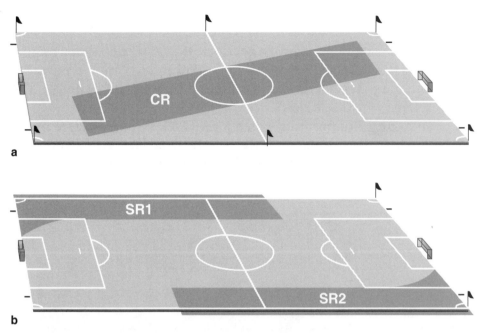

a

b

FIGURE 5.5   Pattern of coverage for *(a)* the center referee and *(b)* side referees in the double-dual (three-whistle) system.

Kickoffs

For kickoffs, the center referee (CR) and the side referees (SR1 and SR2) should be positioned as shown in figure 5.6. The center referee should be ready to move up and down the diagonal, and the side referees should also be prepared to move according to the play, staying even with the second-to-last defender on their side of the field or with the ball, whichever is closer to the goal.

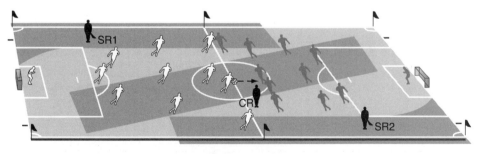

FIGURE 5.6   Positions of officials for a kickoff.

Goal Kicks

A side referee usually signals for a goal kick; the center referee may signal for a goal kick if he or she has a better view of the play. One referee makes the call and another referee confirms the call through eye contact. The center referee whistles, if needed.

For an example of positions when a goal kick is awarded, see figure 5.7. Notice that one side referee (SR2) is on the goal line, in good position to determine whether the ball goes beyond the goal line.

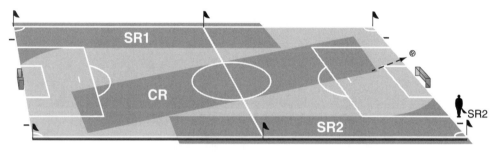

FIGURE 5.7   Positions of officials when awarding a goal kick.

When a goal kick is taken, the positions should be as shown in figure 5.8. Note that the side referee is in line with the outside edge of the penalty area after checking ball placement. The side referee should make sure that the ball leaves the penalty area before being played a second time. The other side referee assumes a position in line with the second-to-last defender and prepares for a possible counterattack by the team taking the goal kick.

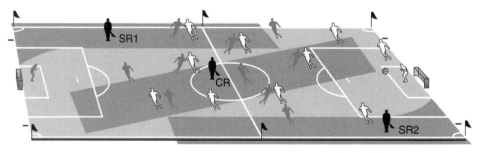

FIGURE 5.8   Positions of officials when a goal kick is taken.

Corner Kicks

A side referee signals for a corner kick if the kick is coming from the near side of the field—that is, the portion that the side referee covers. If the kick is coming from the far side, the center referee is closer to the play and typically would signal for the kick. The positions of the referees for a corner kick are shown in figure 5.9.

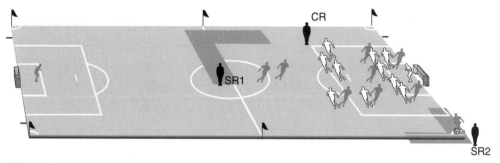

FIGURE 5.9   Positions of officials for a corner kick.

The side referee is on the goal line, between the touchline and the penalty area (see SR2's position in figure 5.9). The center referee is near the far edge of the penalty area, ready to move either toward the center of the field or toward the goal line, depending on how the play develops. The other side referee is in position on the far side of the field, observing the whole field and ready to react to a counterattack.

Penalty Kicks

When a penalty kick is warranted, the official who observes the violation whistles and signals to stop the clock, then quickly gets into position for the kick (see figure 5.10).

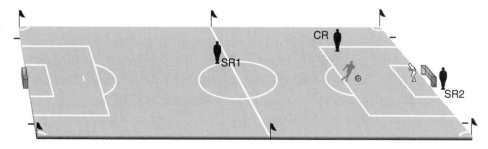

FIGURE 5.10   Positions of officials for a penalty kick.

The side referee is on the goal line, ready to observe whether the ball completely crosses the goal line (see SR2's position in figure 5.10); the center referee is in the penalty area and whistles for the kick to take place. The center referee and the side referee closest to the play observe the kicker and watch for encroachment and movement by the goalkeeper before the kick. The other side referee observes the whole field and prepares for a counterattack.

Free Kicks

Before a free kick, the center referee should move downfield to where he or she thinks the kick might land and observe the attackers and defenders in that area (see figure 5.11).

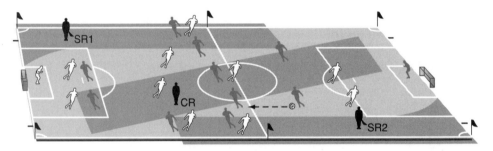

FIGURE 5.11   Positions of officials for a free kick.

The side referee closest to the goal in the direction the kick is being made should move ahead of the ball and be ready to cover the attack, watching for offside and other violations. The other side referee should move off his or her normal pattern of movement and administer the kick. This side referee should administer the kick unless it is deep in the offensive area. In this case, the center referee should administer the kick.

For free kicks near the goal, the side referee nearest to the goal should position himself or herself on the goal line and be prepared to call violations and observe whether a kick goes over the goal line (see SR2's position in figure 5.12). The center referee should watch for offside and other violations, and the other side referee should watch for violations and be ready for a counterattack. All referees should be ready to recover their positions quickly if the play moves back up the field.

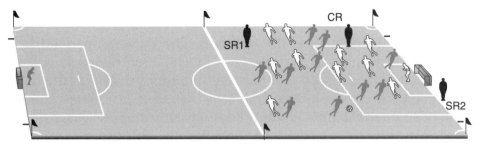

FIGURE 5.12   Positions of officials for a free kick near the goal.

Throw-Ins

A side referee typically indicates when a throw-in is to take place. In restarting play, the side referees and the center referee should be in their normal patterns (see figure 5.13). If a problem develops—for instance, the incorrect team is preparing to throw in, another ball is on the field or the ball is soft—the nearest referee should tend to it.

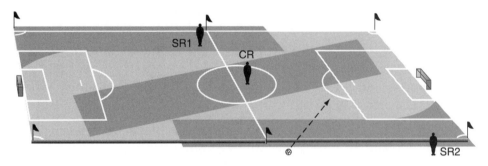

FIGURE 5.13   Positions of officials for a throw-in.

The center referee should observe the players near the area where the throw will likely be going. The side referee nearest the throw observes the thrower, watching for foot faults, hand faults and for the ball properly entering the field. This side referee whistles for play to restart, if needed. The other side referee watches the whole field and is ready for a counterattack, should the ball be taken by the defense and the play redirected toward the opposite goal.

Drop Balls

For a drop ball situation, the two opposing players involved face
their respective goals. Other players can position themselves anywhere on the field, as long as they are not interfering with the drop
ball action. The center referee drops the ball; the side referees should
be in position to call offside should the ball come their way (see figure
5.14). If the drop is near the touchline, the closest side referee should
administer it.

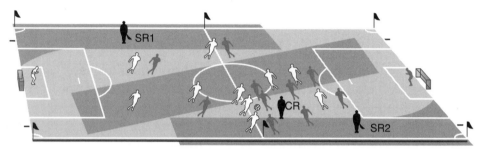

FIGURE 5.14   Positions of officials for a drop ball.

A game is restarted with a drop ball in the following situations:

- When the ball goes out of bounds and it cannot be determined which
  team caused it to go out

- When the ball goes out of bounds and a player from each team
  simultaneously causes the ball to go out

- When the ball becomes deflated or is losing air

- Following a temporary suspension of play and neither team has
  clear possession

- When simultaneous fouls of the same degree occur

The drop ball occurs in the spot on the field where the ball became
dead unless it became dead in the penalty area. If the ball became dead
in the penalty area, it will be dropped from the spot on the goal area line
that is parallel to the goal line at a point where the ball originally went
out of bounds. Additionally, the ball must touch the ground before either
player can touch the ball.

Now that you've been introduced to the three systems of soccer officiating and the mechanics involved with officiating in each system, let's turn to another aspect of refereeing: making calls in game situations. In the next several chapters you'll consider situations that you will face in games and decide how you would rule if confronted with each situation.

PART III

Applying the Rules

CHAPTER 6

PROCEDURES AND CONDUCT

A s you know from your *NFHS Soccer Rules Book*, there are 18 rules: 17 cover the basic aspects of the game, plus Rule 18, which covers definitions. In the next three chapters we'll consider various cases in the 17 main areas. For each rule, we'll present a few case studies and provide the appropriate rulings. These discussions are meant to supplement your close study of the *NFHS Soccer Rules Book* and show you some realistic applications of the rules, but they are not a substitute for thorough knowledge of the *NFHS Soccer Rules Book*. You should use this text to test and augment your understanding of those rules.

In this chapter we'll consider cases in the first six rules:

- Rule 1: The Field of Play
- Rule 2: The Ball
- Rule 3: The Players and Substitutions
- Rule 4: Player Equipment
- Rule 5: The Officials
- Rule 6: Ball Holders, Timer and Scorer

Rule 1: The Field of Play

Rule 1 covers the size of the field, markings, corner flags, goals, official and team areas, spectators' areas and field conditions. Here we'll present several scenarios related to these issues and their rulings. Decide how you would make the call and then check your decision against the answers beginning on page 87.

CASE 1: Field Markings

A game between York and Brownsburg is scheduled to be played on Brownsburg's football field, which is lined for both football and soccer. As you conduct your pregame field inspection, you notice that the soccer playing area and boundary lines are marked with lines that are similar in width, color and markings to those used for football. Can the game be played on this field?

Would your answer change if the soccer lines were marked in a color that contrasted with the football lines, with material that is safe for eyes and skin?

CASE 2: Incorrect Penalty Area Lines

As you inspect the field before a game between Pittsfield and Jamestown, you notice that the penalty area line measurement appears to be off. Your observation is proved correct: The lines extend into the field of play for 16 yards rather than the required 18. What do you do?

CASE 3: Goalpost Placement

As you check the goalposts before a game in Westwood between Centralia and Westwood, you observe that the goalposts are placed in front of the goal line. How do you respond?

What would you do if you found the front edges of the goalposts to be behind the goal line? Would your response be any different if the rear edges of the goalposts were on the outer edge of the goal line?

Rule 2: The Ball

Rule 2 describes legal balls to be used in competition. These specifications include the proper size and weight of the ball, the ball's casing and inflation, the authenticating mark on the ball and what happens if the ball becomes deflated during play. While there are relatively few rules regarding the ball, their importance is obvious. After all, without a regulation ball, there is no game!

Following are two cases taken from Rule 2; decide how you would make the call and then check your decision against the answers beginning on page 88.

CASE 4: Using a Ball That Is Not Authenticated

In a game between Richmond and Brownsburg, there are no balls on site that have the NFHS authenticating mark. What do you do?

CASE 5: Deflated Ball

Westwood is hosting York in a game that is late in the first half with the score 2-1 in York's favor. Westwood is attacking York's goal. A shot by a Westwood player strikes the crossbar and the ball drops to the ground, deflated. Do you allow the players to continue, or do you intercede?

Rule 3: The Players and Substitutions

Rule 3 covers player and substitution procedures, including how many players are needed to begin a game, what to do when too many players are on the field and what are proper and improper substitutions. Following are a few cases taken from Rule 3; decide how you would make the call and then check your decision against the answers beginning on page 88.

CASE 6: Playing Without a Goalkeeper

Late in the game with Richmond trailing Independence, 4-2, the Richmond coach decides to pull her goalkeeper and send in a forward to try to generate some offense. Is this legal?

CASE 7: Twelve Players in the Game

Pittsfield has just scored a goal to go ahead of Westwood, 2-1. However, before the game is restarted after the goal, you notice that Pittsfield had 12 players in the game when the goal was scored. What do you do?

Would your ruling be any different if you had restarted the game before you noticed Pittsfield had 12 players in the game when they scored the goal?

CASE 8: Team Roster Not Filled Out

Before a game against Brownsburg, the Richmond coach tells you that he hasn't yet filled out his team roster. He asks that the game be started and promises to provide the roster at halftime. How do you respond?

CASE 9: Unlisted Player Scoring a Goal

A Jamestown player scores a goal against York. The player who scored is not on Jamestown's roster. You allow the goal, and the York coach argues that the goal shouldn't be allowed because the player was unlisted. Who's right—you or the coach?

CASE 10: Foul Play

A Westwood player fouls an Independence player in the penalty area in a manner that you consider to be unsporting, injuring the Independence player and resulting in a penalty kick. The Westwood player who committed the foul is disqualified because it's her second caution. The Westwood coach substitutes for the disqualified player, and the Independence coach substitutes for her injured player, with the new player preparing to take the penalty kick. Is everything legal?

Officials must be extra alert for fouls that are unsporting and make calls appropriately.

Rule 4: Player Equipment

Player cleats, uniforms, shinguards and other equipment are addressed in Rule 4. Following are a few cases taken from Rule 4; decide how you would make the call and then check your decision against the answers beginning on page 89.

CASE 11: Baseball Cleats—Legal or Not?

In a game between Pittsfield and Brownsburg, you notice that a Browns-burg player is wearing baseball cleats. Is this legal?

Would your ruling be different if the player were wearing track shoes with spikes? How about turf shoes, metal cleats or plastic cleats?

CASE 12: Teammates Wearing the Same Number

In a game at Richmond, the Centralia coach wants to send in a substitute, wearing number 22, for another player (number 10). However, Centralia already has a player with number 22 on the field. Should you allow the substitution?

What if number 22 were coming in for number 22? Would your ruling be different?

CASE 13: Removing Shinguards

A Jamestown player removes her shinguards in the second half of a hot and humid game against Independence. As she runs by her team bench, she tosses them off the field and continues to play. Is this legal?

CASE 14: A Knee Brace Reaction

The padding on a York player's knee brace comes loose and falls off during play against Pittsfield. The York player continues to play. Should you immediately stop the action and remove the player until he replaces the padding?

Rule 5: The Officials

This rule covers general rules concerning the officials, including pregame, game and postgame responsibilities. Following are a few cases taken from Rule 5; decide how you would make the call and then check your decision against the answers beginning on page 90.

CASE 15: Agreeing to Bend the Rules

A Centralia player is disqualified for abusive language in a game against Brownsburg. Centralia has a limited number of substitutes, and the Brownsburg coach, who is old friends with the Centralia coach, says it's OK with her for Centralia to replace the disqualified player. Should you allow the substitution?

CASE 16: Throw-In by Wrong Team

You clearly signal that Westwood is entitled to a throw-in against Jamestown. However, a Jamestown player picks up the ball and makes a throw-in to a teammate. You recognize the error immediately after the ball is put in play. What do you do?

CASE 17: A Handy Play

A Richmond player shoots on goal in the penalty area, and an Independence fullback reaches out and deflects the ball with his hands. The Richmond player recovers the ball, kicks again and scores. Does the goal stand, or do you have a call to make before the goal?

Would your ruling be any different if, in the same situation, the Richmond player *didn't* score?

CASE 18: Unsporting Conduct or Not?

Near the end of the first half of a game between York and Centralia, you caution the York coach for unsporting conduct. As the first half comes to a close, the York coach continues to indicate his dissatisfaction, both verbally and by gestures. How do you respond?

CASE 19: Advantage Play

A Pittsfield player is deliberately tripped by a Brownsburg defender just outside Brownsburg's penalty area. Because the Pittsfield team has an advantage that does not appear to have been taken away by the foul, you signal and call, "Play on!" The Pittsfield player, who has maintained control of the ball, then stumbles and falls to the ground. What do you call?

Would your call be different if the Pittsfield player had maintained control and sailed a shot wide of the goal? What if she had continued and was immediately fouled again, this time inside the penalty area?

Rule 6: Ball Holders, Timer and Scorer

Rule 6 details the duties of ball holders, the timer and the scorer, and describes how you should communicate with them. Following are a few cases taken from Rule 6; decide how you would make the call and then check your decision against the answers beginning on page 91.

CASE 20: Who's Got the Time?
Westwood is playing at Richmond. Before the game begins, Richmond officials request that the head referee keep time. How do you respond?

Answers

Here you'll find the answers to the questions in this chapter. For any answers that you missed, check your *NFHS Soccer Rules Book* and make sure you understand the ruling before you go out to officiate your next game. The more thoroughly you know the rules, the more comfortable you'll be on the field, as you'll be ready to make any call.

Case 1: Field Markings
It is recommended that you play the game and report the problem afterward to the proper authorities. If the field is marked in a contrasting color with safe material, this is both legal and ideal. The ideal situation is a field dedicated to soccer without any additional markings, because even contrasting colors can be confusing in situations where there are areas of shadow or in low-light conditions.

Case 2: Incorrect Penalty Area Lines
The game can be played with the lines incorrectly marked, but you should advise the home team's coach that the error must be corrected before their next home game. In addition, report this incident to the proper authorities—the state association, the local association, the tournament director or the host school.

Case 3: Goalpost Placement
If the goalposts are placed in front of the goal line, this is improper placement, and the game can't be played until the error is corrected either by moving the goals or by re-marking the goal line. Notify the Westwood coach and game management to rectify the situation.

You should do the same if you find that the front edges of the goalposts are behind the goal line. If, however, you find the rear edge of the goalposts to be on the outer edge of the goal line, this is considered correct placement.

Case 4: Using a Ball That Is Not Authenticated

You should play the game using the balls that are available, then report the lack of authenticated balls to the proper authority. Game balls are required to include the NFHS authenticating mark, but you don't have to cancel a game if such balls aren't available.

Case 5: Deflated Ball

You should declare the ball dead where it became a dead ball. Get another official game ball from Westwood and resume the game with a drop ball between any two opposing players at the spot where it became a dead ball. In this case, as the ball became dead within the goal area, drop the ball on the goal area line that runs parallel to the goal line nearest to where the ball was when it was last played.

All goalkeepers, even those entering the game as a substitute, must be properly attired.

Case 6: Playing Without a Goalkeeper

Yes, the Richmond coach can pull her goalkeeper and substitute a field player for her. However, Richmond still needs to keep a designated, properly attired goalkeeper on the field.

Case 7: Twelve Players in the Game

You should not allow the goal. However, had the game restarted, you would have had to let the goal stand. In both instances, the twelfth player would be removed from the game and cautioned. In the first case, the restart would be a goal kick since the ball crossed the goal line last touched by an attacking player. In the second case, the restart would depend on how the game had been stopped once the referee recognized the error. If the game was stopped solely to remove the twelfth player and administer the caution, the proper restart would be an indirect free kick for the other team.

Case 8: Team Roster Not Filled Out
You should respond by telling the Richmond coach that the game can't start until he has filled out his roster and turned it in. A match cannot start until you have received rosters from each team. Teams may also exchange rosters, but this isn't required.

Case 9: Unlisted Player Scoring a Goal
You're right; the goal should be allowed. Because teams can add players to the roster after the start of play, you should allow a goal by a player who is not on the roster. The team should add the player's name to the roster.

Case 10: Foul Play
No, everything isn't legal. The substitutions are appropriate, but the new Independence player can't take the penalty kick.

Case 11: Baseball Cleats—Legal or Not?
The Brownsburg player wearing the baseball cleats is doing so illegally. The player should not be allowed to play until he puts on legal shoes—which include turf shoes, metal cleats or plastic cleats (but not track shoes with spikes), as long as you determine that those shoes are safe.

Case 12: Teammates Wearing the Same Number
No, you should not allow the substitution. Two players on the same team can't have the same number. If you spot the problem after allowing the player to enter, you should stop the game and have the player leave the game as soon as you discover the duplicate number. You should verify which of the players should be number 22 based on the roster and make sure that the other player has the correct number per the roster before he re-enters the game.

Case 13: Removing Shinguards
No, the Jamestown player may not remove her shinguards. You should stop the action and ask the player to leave the field, then inspect the player's shinguards before you allow her to re-enter. Players must wear shinguards that provide reasonable protection for their shins.

Case 14: A Knee Brace Reaction

You don't need to stop play and remove the York player unless you deem that the unpadded brace presents an immediate danger. If you believe there is no immediate danger, then wait for the next stoppage of play and ask the player to leave the field to correct the problem.

Case 15: Agreeing to Bend the Rules

No, you shouldn't allow Centralia to substitute for their disqualified player, even if the Brownsburg coach is willing to bend the rules. Coaches have no authority to bend the rules of the game, and neither do officials.

Case 16: Throw-In by Wrong Team

Because Jamestown was not entitled to the throw-in, stop the action and award the throw-in to Westwood after cautioning the Jamestown player who made the throw-in for unsporting conduct. If you view the actions of the player as a misunderstanding, there is no need for the caution.

Case 17: A Handy Play

Because the Richmond player recovered the ball and scored, you should allow the goal even though the Independence fullback handled the ball. Had the Richmond player not scored, you should have called handling and awarded a penalty kick. In either case, you should disqualify the Independence fullback for serious foul play.

Case 18: Unsporting Conduct or Not?

You should respond by disqualifying the York coach and having him removed from the vicinity of the playing area. The York coach is prohibited for the rest of the game from further contact, direct or indirect, with team members. If the coach doesn't comply with this, you should terminate the game. The incident should be reported in writing to the proper authorities. Note: As required by your state association, if there is not a responsible adult present to supervise the team, the game should be terminated.

Case 19: Advantage Play

Pittsfield was in an advantage situation and you correctly signaled and called out to play on. However, because the advantage did not materialize, you should penalize Brownsburg for the foul and award a direct free kick to Pittsfield.

Had the Pittsfield player gotten a shot off that sailed wide of the goal, you wouldn't enforce any penalty, although you could come back and caution or even disqualify the player who tripped the attacker if you believe that the act of tripping was sanctionable misconduct. If the Pittsfield player is fouled again, this time in the penalty area, you should ignore the previous advantage situation and award a penalty kick to Pittsfield.

Case 20: Who's Got the Time?

If the Richmond school officials request that the head referee keep time, and the Westwood and Richmond coaches agree to this, then the head referee can keep time. (However, check with your state association; some associations may require that time must be kept by the timer, unless a visible clock is not available, in which case it can be kept by the referee.)

CHAPTER 7

PLAY

In chapter 6 we presented play rulings for the first six rules of soccer. In this chapter we'll present rulings for the next six rules:

- Rule 7: Duration of the Game and Length of Periods
- Rule 8: The Start of Play
- Rule 9: Ball In and Out of Play
- Rule 10: Scoring
- Rule 11: Offside
- Rule 12: Fouls and Misconduct

Again, for each rule we'll present case studies and provide the appropriate rulings. See how you do in making your calls, and continue to thoroughly study your *NFHS Soccer Rules Book*.

Rule 7: Duration of the Game and Length of Periods

Rule 7 details game length and takes into consideration rulings involving time expiring, intervals between periods, tie games, time-outs and time-ins, and terminated games. Following are a few cases taken from Rule 7; decide how you would make the call and then check your decision against the answers beginning on page 99.

CASE 1: Terminating a Game

York, playing at Pittsfield, is leading 2-0 late in the first half. The Pittsfield fans, who have been unruly the entire game, cause enough disturbance late in the first half that you terminate the game due to spectator interference, declaring York to be the winner. Is this legal?

CASE 2: Penalty Kick When Time Expires

In a game between Jamestown and Brownsburg, a Jamestown player is awarded a penalty kick as time expires. The player takes the kick, and the Brownsburg goalkeeper deflects the ball, which is then shot into the goal by a teammate of the Jamestown player who took the penalty kick. What's the call?

Would your call be any different if there had been two seconds remaining on the clock when Jamestown took the penalty kick and a Jamestown player kicked the deflected ball into the net before time expired?

Officials should refer to Rule 8 for information on the procedures and mechanics for starting a game.

Rule 8: The Start of Play

Rule 8 addresses the procedures for starting play with a kickoff. Following is a case taken from Rule 8; decide how you would make the call and then check your decision against the answer on page 100.

CASE 3: Goal on the Kickoff

Centralia is kicking off in a game against Richmond. It had rained earlier in the afternoon and the grass is still slick. A strong wind is blowing toward the Richmond goal. The player kicking off for Centralia drills a long shot down the field and the ball skips low on the wet grass, eluding the goalkeeper and going into the net. Besides the Centralia player kicking off, no one else has touched the ball. Is the goal allowed?

Rule 9: Ball In and Out of Play

Procedures and rules covering when the ball is in and out of play, including drop ball situations and temporary suspensions, are considered in Rule 9. Following are a few cases taken from Rule 9; decide how you would make the call and then check your decision against the answers beginning on page 100.

CASE 4: Pass Striking Referee

A Westwood player passes to a teammate in a game against Independence, but the pass strikes you while you are in the field. Though the pass appeared to be well placed for the Westwood player's teammate, as the ball deflects off you it goes to an Independence player, who controls the ball. Is this legal?

Would your ruling change if the pass had struck you while you were straddling the touchline, with the ball remaining inbounds, or while you were out of bounds?

CASE 5: Indirect Free Kick Striking Referee

Pittsfield has been awarded an indirect free kick against Brownsburg. The kick strikes you and then deflects directly into the goal. Do you award the goal?

Would your ruling change if the kick struck you and deflected to an onside Pittsfield player who then kicked the ball in the goal?

CASE 6: At the Drop of a Ball

The ball is loose within the goal area in a game between Jamestown and Westwood; neither team is in control of the ball. As players from both teams are running after the ball, a Westwood player crumples to the ground with an injury. How do you respond?

Would your response be any different if the ball were outside the goal area but within the penalty area?

CASE 7: Stopping Play

A Richmond forward takes a shot on goal that is stopped by a York fullback, but in stopping the ball the York player is injured. The ball is recovered by a York teammate, who begins downfield with the ball. Is there any call to make?

CASE 8: Inadvertent Whistle

During a game between Independence and Centralia, you inadvertently sound your whistle. Independence was in control of the ball at the time of the whistle. What should you do?

Rule 10: Scoring

Rule 10 details when a goal is legal and other matters concerning scoring. Following are two cases taken from Rule 10; decide how you would make the call and then check your decision against the answers beginning on page 101.

CASE 9: Scoring on a Throw-In

In a game between Brownsburg and Richmond, you award a throw-in to Brownsburg. A Brownsburg player throws in to a teammate, but the ball goes past all players—including the Richmond goalkeeper, who wasn't expecting the ball to come his way. The ball goes into the goal without touching a player. Should the goal be allowed?

CASE 10: Putting It All on the Line

A Westwood player shoots on goal against York, and the ball rolls along the goal line, between the goalposts, before the goalkeeper manages to fist the ball into the field of play. Has Westwood scored a goal?

Rule 11: Offside

Rule 11 describes the differences between players who are in an offside position and may remain there legally and players who should be sanctioned for being in an offside position. Following are a few cases taken from Rule 11; decide how you would make the call and then check your decision against the answers beginning on page 102.

CASE 11: Stepping Out

After an attack on goal that has been repelled by the Jamestown defense, and with the ball controlled by Jamestown and going back up the field, an Independence player lingers downfield, near the touchline. The ball is intercepted by Independence, and the action is coming down the touchline where the Independence player is, with only the goalkeeper nearer to the goal line than the Independence player. The pass is made to an Independence player who is not in the offside position. The Independence player who was in the offside position steps off the field, hoping to avoid the offside call. What do you call?

CASE 12: Offside but Not in the Play

A Pittsfield player is in an offside position, with only the goalkeeper between her and the Centralia goal, as one of her teammates is dribbling the ball near midfield in the offensive half of the field. The player in the offside position is just outside the penalty area and is making no attempt to enter into the play, and her teammate does not pass to her. Is there an offside violation?

CASE 13: An Offside Trap

Richmond is attacking on the offensive end of the field against Westwood. As a Richmond player dribbles toward the penalty area, his teammates fill support positions on the sides. The Westwood defenders move forward, placing the Richmond support players in an offside position. Rather than defend the ball, they are waiting for an offside call from you, and it's true that the Richmond players are now in an offside position. Meanwhile, the Richmond player with the ball near the penalty area dribbles in a little closer, shoots and scores. Is it a goal or is it offside?

CASE 14: Offside on a Drop Ball

A York player who is in an offside position receives the ball in a drop ball situation directly after it has been kicked by a Brownsburg player. Should you call offside?

Would your call change if the York player, still in an offside position, had received a pass directly from one of her teammates?

Rule 12: Fouls and Misconduct

Rule 12 covers a variety of fouls and misconduct on the field, such as spitting, striking and kicking; handling the ball; holding and pushing; charging; obstruction; dangerous play; goalkeeper restriction and various other types of misconduct. Following are a few cases taken from Rule 12; decide how you would make the call and then check your decision against the answers beginning on page 102.

CASE 15: An Intentional, but Missed, Foul
Throughout a game between Jamestown and Pittsfield there has been bad blood between two opposing players. It started when a Jamestown player unintentionally tripped a Pittsfield player. Now, late in the second half, the Pittsfield player, who has been frustrated the whole game by the rough tactics of the Jamestown player, attempts to trip the player. The Jamestown player steps over the trip and no contact occurs. Is there any call to make?

CASE 16: Getting a Handle on Things
A Centralia player is in a defensive position during a free kick taken by Richmond. The Centralia player places his hands to protect his groin before the kick is taken. The Richmond player drills the ball and it strikes the Centralia player's hands, which haven't moved. Is there a penalty to be called?

CASE 17: Not a Heady Play
Late in the first half of a tie game against Independence, a Westwood player performs a diving header in an attempt to score. As he dives for the ball, an Independence defender, in attempting to play the ball, kicks the diving Westwood player in the head. What's the call?

CASE 18: A Handy Goalkeeper
York attempts a shot on goal, and the Jamestown goalkeeper deflects the ball to the ground. She begins to dribble the ball with her feet to the edge of the penalty area, where she stops, picks up the ball and distributes it to a teammate. Is this legal?

Would your call be any different if the goalkeeper had deflected the ball, then scrambled to pick it up and distribute it to a teammate without dribbling it?

CASE 19: Verbal Deception

A Brownsburg player is waiting to receive a ball in the air when a Pittsfield player who is behind the Brownsburg player screams in the Brownsburg player's ear in an obvious attempt to distract her. The Brownsburg player lets the ball go past her and it is received by the Pittsfield player. Do you have a call to make?

CASE 20: Taunting or Not?

Midway through the second half of a tightly contested game between Independence and Centralia, you caution an Independence player. As that player is leaving the field, a Centralia player goes up to the Independence player and sarcastically applauds. The Centralia player follows the Independence player toward the sideline, continuing to applaud. What's the call?

Answers

Following are the answers to the questions posed in this chapter. For any answers that you missed, check your rules book and make sure you understand the ruling before you go out to officiate your next game. Remember, the more thoroughly you know the rules, the more comfortable you'll be on the field, as you'll be ready to make any call.

Case 1: Terminating a Game

You can terminate a game for spectator interference, but you can't declare a winner in a terminated game. Your responsibility is to report the situation to the state association; it's within their jurisdiction to determine the outcome of the game.

Case 2: Penalty Kick When Time Expires

The goal kicked in by the teammate does not count because time had expired and no kick after the penalty kick itself can count. If, however, two seconds remained and the teammate had kicked the ball in before time expired, the goal would count.

Case 3: Goal on the Kickoff

The Centralia goal counts. Once you signal with your whistle that play is to begin, it is each player's responsibility to be ready to play. No other player has to touch the ball on a kickoff for a goal to be scored.

Case 4: Pass Striking Referee

There is no call to make when the ball strikes a referee who is inbounds. Independence, therefore, is the recipient of a lucky bounce.

Had the ball struck you and remained in the field while you were straddling the touchline, it should have remained in play with no call being made. Had it struck you while you were out of bounds, you should have awarded a throw-in to Independence, providing the ball passed completely over the touchline. It is the position of the ball, and not of the referee, that determines whether the ball is in or out of play.

Case 5: Indirect Free Kick Striking Referee

You should not award Pittsfield a goal on an indirect free kick that deflects off you into the goal, because the ball didn't touch another player. Restart the game with a goal kick.

If the ball deflected off you to another Pittsfield player who is onside, and that player kicks the ball in, the goal counts, because another player played the ball. Remember, the ball is in play when it rebounds from or strikes an official in the field of play.

Case 6: At the Drop of a Ball

You should stop the game for the injured player. Once the player is removed from the game, restart it with a drop ball at the nearest spot on that part of the goal area line that runs parallel to the goal line. When stopping play for an injury, the game situation should be considered, but err on the side of caution for the protection of the players.

If the ball had been outside the goal area but within the penalty area, you would have restarted play with a drop ball at the place where the ball was when you suspended play.

Case 7: Stopping Play

With the injury to the York player, you should stop the game and award an indirect free kick to York because they were in possession of the ball when you stopped the game.

Case 8: Inadvertent Whistle

Even though the whistle was inadvertent, you need to stop play in order to avoid giving one team an unfair advantage. Because Independence was in control of the ball at the time of the whistle, you should award them an indirect free kick. If neither team had been in control, you would have had a drop ball situation.

Case 9: Scoring on a Throw-In
No, you should not allow the goal. A goal cannot be scored directly from a throw-in. Play would restart with a goal kick by Richmond.

Case 10: Putting It All on the Line
No, Westwood hasn't scored a goal. The entire ball has to pass beyond the goal line for that to happen.

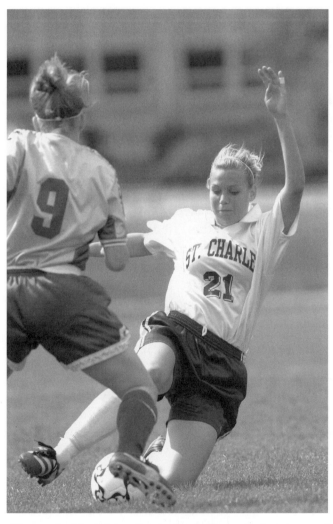

After a shot is taken, the entire ball must pass beyond the goal line in order to be counted as a goal.

Case 11: Stepping Out

You should call nothing, because the Independence player is not offside until he interferes with play or gains an advantage. A player can step off the field to avoid being called offside by the referee as long as that player doesn't distract an opponent or aid a teammate.

Case 12: Offside but Not in the Play

No, the Pittsfield player is not offside because she made no attempt to enter into the play and was not involved in it. If her teammate had passed her the ball, then you would call offside.

Case 13: An Offside Trap

The Richmond goal should be allowed. The teammates who were trapped into an offside position did not participate in the play. If, however, one of the players "caught" in the trap becomes involved in the play, he would be offside.

Case 14: Offside on a Drop Ball

The York player should not be called for offside when receiving the ball directly from a Brownsburg player in a drop ball situation. Of course, if the offside York player had received a pass from a teammate, she should have been whistled for offside.

Case 15: An Intentional, but Missed, Foul

Yes, there's a call to make—the Pittsfield player attempted to trip the Jamestown player, and this attempt is illegal even though it wasn't successful. You should stop play and award a direct free kick to Jamestown, unless you choose to invoke the advantage clause. Depending on the nature of the attempt and your sense of the need for game-control actions, you might also choose to caution the Pittsfield player for unsporting conduct.

Case 16: Getting a Handle on Things

There is no handling call to make because the Centralia player had his hands in place before the kick and did not move them to play the ball. Had he moved them during the kick to protect himself, and had the ball struck his hands or arms, then he would have committed a handling violation.

Case 17: Not a Heady Play

You should give Independence an indirect free kick. Though the Westwood player came out on the worse end, he created his own dangerous situation by attempting to head a ball that he could reasonably expect to be kicked. The Independence player has the right to try to play the ball.

Case 18: A Handy Goalkeeper

No, this is not legal. The Jamestown goalkeeper cannot pick up the ball after parrying it. You should award an indirect free kick to York.

If the goalkeeper had deflected the ball and then picked it up without dribbling it, this would be OK because the deflection is considered an unintentional action.

Case 19: Verbal Deception

Yes, you do have a call to make. You should stop play, caution the Pittsfield player for unsporting conduct and restart play with an indirect free kick for Jamestown at the spot of the violation.

Case 20: Taunting or Not?

You should disqualify the Centralia player for taunting. The Centralia team can substitute for the disqualified player.

CHAPTER 8

KICKS

In this chapter we'll continue to explore rules, presenting scenarios in which you decide the proper calls to make. We'll look at Rules 13 through 17, which address certain special restarts.

- Rule 13: Free Kick
- Rule 14: Penalty Kick
- Rule 15: Throw-In
- Rule 16: Goal Kick
- Rule 17: Corner Kick

Rule 13: Free Kick

Rule 13 defines direct and indirect free kicks. It discusses when free kicks are awarded and describes the proper procedures for taking them. Following are a few cases taken from Rule 13; decide how you would make the call and then check your decision against the answers beginning on page 110.

CASE 1: A Trick Kick
You have just awarded a free kick to Centralia in a game against Richmond. As a Centralia player approaches the ball to take the kick, she steps over the ball at the last moment and a teammate kicks the ball. The Richmond coach shouts out that this maneuver is illegal. Is the Richmond coach correct?

CASE 2: Direct or Indirect Free Kick?
You have just penalized a Westwood player for obstructing the Independence goalkeeper, a member of the defending team, near the right goalpost. What type of kick do you award, and where is that kick to be taken?

CASE 3: Goal or No Goal?

A Pittsfield defender commits a dangerous play against a Brownsburg player inside the Pittsfield goal area. A Brownsburg player places the ball at the point of the foul and plays it to a teammate, who scores. Does the goal count?

CASE 4: A Quick Kick

Jamestown is attacking in Westwood's half of the field, about 35 yards from the goal, when a Westwood player trips the Jamestown player who is dribbling the ball. The offense is a nonviolent one. You whistle for the foul and signal for a direct free kick to be taken by Jamestown.

A Jamestown player, seeing the chance to gain an advantage, rushes up and kicks the ball within two seconds of your whistle. Because of the quick reaction by the Jamestown player who took the kick, the Westwood player who committed the foul is standing within 4 yards of the ball when it is kicked. The Westwood player neither makes an attempt to move back the required yardage nor attempts to play the ball once it is kicked. However, he in effect acts as a one-man wall, and the ball strikes him, negating any advantage the Jamestown player was hoping to gain through the quick kick. Is this legal?

Would your response change if the Westwood player had been retreating as he was struck by the ball, but he still had not been trying to play it? What if he stuck out a leg and deflected the ball on purpose?

Rule 14: Penalty Kick

Rule 14 defines what a penalty kick is and when and how it should be taken. It also describes various penalty-kick situations. Following are a few cases taken from Rule 14; decide how you would make the call and then check your decision against the answers beginning on page 110.

CASE 5: Penalty Kick Position

You have just awarded a penalty kick to York. As the players are lining up for the kick, you notice that a Richmond player is lined up five yards from the goal line. How do you respond to this situation?

CASE 6: Encroachment

An Independence player is about to take a penalty kick against Centralia when a teammate of the kicker encroaches. The Independence player follows through with her kick, which is saved and held by the Centralia goalkeeper. Do you have a call to make?

What if, on a penalty kick, the Centralia goalkeeper lunges forward just before the kick is taken, but a goal is scored? Does the goal count?

A penalty kick is awarded when a foul occurs within the offending team's penalty area.

CASE 7: Two Players Kicking the Ball

Brownsburg has been awarded a penalty kick against Richmond. The Brownsburg player taking the kick rushes forward, but in his anxiety he miskicks and the ball dribbles forward. An alert teammate steps in and fires a shot on goal, drilling it past the goalkeeper. Does the goal count?

Would your decision be different if the first Brownsburg player rushed up and then deliberately paused before kicking the ball into the net?

CASE 8: Goal After Time Expired

Westwood has been awarded a penalty kick against York after time has expired. The Westwood player approaches and kicks the ball toward a corner of the goal, but the York goalkeeper dives and deflects the ball. The ball continues to roll and it crosses the goal line before the goalkeeper can scramble to his feet and stop it. Is this a goal?

Rule 15: Throw-In

Rule 15 describes when a throw-in should be awarded and covers the required elements of a proper throw-in. Decide how you would make the call and then check your decision against the answers beginning on page 112.

CASE 9: Throw-In From the Wrong Spot

Independence is awarded a throw-in against Jamestown near the halfway line. The Independence player making the throw-in releases the ball five yards farther up the touchline than where it went into touch. What's the call?

CASE 10: A Running Throw-In

In a game against Centralia, a Pittsfield player who is executing a throw-in takes a run up to the touchline and releases the ball at the proper location while both feet are on the ground. Is this legal?

Would your answer be different if the Pittsfield player had lifted one of her feet off the ground as she made the throw-in? What if she had both feet on the ground, but one was touching the touchline during the throw-in while the other foot was out of bounds?

CASE 11: Defending Against a Throw-In

You have just awarded a throw-in to Richmond in a game against Westwood. As a Richmond player is about to make the throw-in, a Westwood defender rushes up and stands directly on the touchline where the throw-in is to be made. Is this legal?

What if the Westwood defender had positioned himself in the same spot on the touchline *before* the Richmond player began his throw-in? Would that make any difference?

Rule 16: Goal Kick

Rule 16 details when a goal kick should be awarded and how the kick should be taken, including the limitations on the defending team and legal play directly following the kick. Decide how you would make the call and then check your decision against the answer on page 113.

CASE 12: Placement of the Goal Kick

Brownsburg has kicked the ball out of bounds beyond York's goal line. Brownsburg's shot on goal missed wide right. Where does the resulting goal kick for York need to be taken from?

Rule 17: Corner Kick

Rule 17 addresses when a corner kick should be awarded and the procedures for taking the kick, as well as any penalties for violations during the kick. Decide how you would make the call and then check your decision against the answer on page 113.

CASE 13: Playing the Corner Kick

Jamestown has been awarded a corner kick in a game against Pittsfield. The Jamestown player who takes the corner kick hits the goalpost with the kick; the ball rebounds back toward the corner and the same Jamestown player who took the kick plays the ball again before it has been touched by another player. Is this legal?

Answers

Check your responses against the following answers. If you missed any answers, check the relevant rules in the *NFHS Soccer Rules Book*. Prepare well, and good luck in making all the right calls during your games!

Case 1: A Trick Kick

No, the Richmond coach is not correct in saying that the Centralia player cannot step over the ball and allow a teammate to take the free kick instead. The play is legal as long as no Richmond player is within 10 yards of the ball until it is kicked.

Case 2: Direct or Indirect Free Kick?

Independence should get an indirect free kick, and it can be taken anywhere in the goal area. Any time a free kick is awarded to the defending team within its own goal area, the kick can be taken from any point within the goal area.

Case 3: Goal or No Goal?

The Brownsburg goal should not be allowed; Brownsburg should retake the kick. Free kicks awarded to a team inside the opponent's goal area must be taken from the part of the goal area line that runs parallel to the goal line at the point nearest to where the foul was committed.

Case 4: A Quick Kick

There is no penalty to be called when the quick kick strikes the Westwood player. He didn't have time to retreat the required 10 yards, and he didn't attempt to play the ball. Likewise, if he had been attempting to retreat but had been struck by the ball before he was the required distance away, there would be no penalty as long as he did not try to play the ball. However, if he sticks a leg out or in any other way attempts to play the ball and does touch it before he is 10 or more yards away, then he should be cautioned for encroachment and Jamestown gets another kick.

Case 5: Penalty Kick Position

Delay the kick and instruct the Richmond player to move back behind the penalty mark and to stay outside the penalty area at least 10 yards from the ball. All players except the kicker and the goalkeeper must be outside the penalty area, at least 10 yards from the ball and behind the penalty mark, until the ball is kicked.

Case 6: Encroachment

The save by the Centralia goalkeeper stands as is. There's no need to stop play, but at the next stoppage in play you should caution the Independence player who encroached.

Forward movement by a goalkeeper is not allowed before a ball is in play.

In the case of a goalkeeper who lunges forward before the kick is taken in an attempt to stop a goal, but the goal is scored anyway, the goal is allowed. Once the kick is taken, the goalkeeper can lunge forward, but forward movement is not allowed before the ball is in play.

Case 7: Two Players Kicking the Ball

Provided that the second player was correctly positioned prior to the first kick being taken, there is nothing illegal in his kick of his teammate's misfired penalty kick; the Brownsburg goal counts. However, the second situation, where the Brownsburg player intentionally duped the Richmond goalkeeper, stopping abruptly before kicking a goal, is not legal. Brownsburg must retake the kick.

Case 8: Goal After Time Expired

The Westwood goal counts. It doesn't matter that time had expired; the penalty kick is not over until the ball stops, until it goes out of bounds, or until it is retouched by the kicker or one of his teammates.

Case 9: Throw-In From the Wrong Spot

The throw-in must be taken from the point where it crossed the touchline. Because Independence did not take the throw-in from the designated point, you should stop play and award a throw-in to Jamestown at the spot where the ball originally crossed the touchline.

Case 10: A Running Throw-In

There's nothing wrong with the Pittsfield player taking a running throw-in, as long as she runs up to the designated spot, has both feet planted and makes the throw with neither foot beyond the touchline and on the playing field. So if one foot was on the touchline, but not beyond it and on the playing field, and the other foot was out of bounds, the throw-in would still be legal. (For that matter, both feet could be planted on, but not beyond, the touchline, and the throw would still be legal.) If, however, she had lifted a foot off the ground while making the throw-in, a throw-in should be awarded to Centralia at the location where the ball originally went into touch (an illegal throw-in is not a foul).

Case 11: Defending Against a Throw-In

The Westwood player cannot interfere with the actions of a player who is making a throw-in. So you should caution the Westwood player for unsporting conduct. However, if the Westwood player had established his position before the Richmond player began to make his throw-in, there would be no penalty provided; he just stands there and does not make an attempt to interfere with the throw by jumping, waving, etc.

Case 12: Placement of the Goal Kick

York is not restricted to taking the kick near where the ball went beyond the goal line; the goal kick may be taken from anywhere within the goal area. The ball needs to clear the penalty area and enter the field of play.

Case 13: Playing the Corner Kick

No, it's not legal for the Jamestown player to play his own corner kick before anyone else has touched the ball. You should award an indirect free kick to Pittsfield.

NFHS Officiating Soccer Signals

Direct Free Kick

Direct Free Kick

Kicking

Tripping

Holding

Handling

Pushing

Striking

Jumping At

Reckless or
Dangerous Charging

Indirect Free Kick

Indirect Free Kick

Dangerous Play

Obstruction

Offside—Near

Offside—Middle

Offside—Far

Goalkeeper Violation
or Second Touching

General

Play On

Dead Ball

Time-Out

Penalty, Corner
or Goal Kick

a

b

Goal
(a) stop time and *(b)* point to center of field

Start Clock

No Goal

Caution or Ejection

GLOSSARY

advantage—A discretionary judgment in which you permit play to continue rather than stopping play to administer the foul. This concept is based on the premise that the foul did not put the offended team at a disadvantage, or the foul, if called, may take away a favorable opportunity for the offended team. You can subsequently call the foul if the advantage does not materialize.

air dribble—A maneuver by the goalkeeper whereby he or she tosses the ball in the air and takes one or more steps before catching the ball. While the ball is in the air, he or she is considered to be in control of the ball and it cannot be played by an opponent.

bench personnel—Anyone within the team area.

charge—An act by a defensive player using body contact to cause an offensive player to lose or give up possession of the ball. A fair charge must have all the elements present that are set down in the rules. (Players can make shoulder-to-shoulder contact in an upright position, within playing distance of the ball, while having at least one foot on the ground and their arms held close to their body.) An unfair charge has one or more of these elements absent.

defense—The team not in possession of the ball. A team remains on defense until it establishes possession of the ball.

deliberate foul—A planned act intended to disrupt the game and to gain an advantage.

diagonal system of control—A system of officiating that uses one referee on the field who is assisted by two assistant referees. The referee has the sole responsibility to penalize infractions of the rules.

dribbler—An offensive player in control of the ball who attempts to move the ball by periodic touches with the feet.

drop ball—A method by which a dead ball becomes alive. An official drops the ball to the ground. When the ball strikes the ground, it becomes alive and may be played by anyone.

dual system of control—A system of officiating that uses two officials on the field with equal authority to penalize infractions of the rules.

encroachment—The act, by one or more defenders, of advancing within 10 yards of the ball before the taking of a free kick.

excessive celebration—Any delayed, excessive or prolonged act by which one or more players focus attention on themselves or prohibit a timely restart of the game.

forfeit—The loss of a game because of termination (a team has less than seven players), or for any other reason, as determined by the proper authority.

foul—A rule infraction for which a penalty is prescribed.

free kick—A method by which a dead ball becomes alive. The ball is placed on the ground, and, while motionless, it is kicked unchallenged in any direction before being touched by another player. The ball is considered to have moved when it is touched by the kicker's foot.

goal line—The field's shorter boundary lines at the end of the field. The entire line is within the field of play.

goalkeeper—The only designated player of each team who may handle the ball, but only within his or her own penalty area.

hitch kick (scissors kick)—A maneuver in which a kicker's feet leave the ground with the feet usually at a higher elevation than the head.

kicker—A player who attempts to, or does, kick the ball.

live ball—A term that indicates that the ball has been legally kicked or thrown by a player, or dropped by an official, and is in play.

offense (attacking team)—The team that is in possession of the ball.

parrying—The deliberate attempt by the goalkeeper to control or deflect or push the ball down or out with the hands or arms.

pass—The movement of the ball from one player to another by foot, head or other portion of the body (other than the hand).

player—A team member who occupies a position on the field of play during the game. A substitute becomes a player when he or she is beckoned onto the field of play by an official, at which point the replaced individual is no longer a player.

playing distance—The distance between the player and the ball that the official judges to be adequate to control the ball. It will seldom exceed two steps (six feet).

possession—A live ball controlled by a team, player or goalkeeper. A controlled ball is one that can be passed, thrown, dribbled or shot on goal by a player.

serious foul play—A play in which a player commits one of the offenses punishable with a direct free kick (or penalty kick if the offense takes place in the penalty area) and uses disproportionate and unnecessary force when playing for the ball against an opponent.

shielding—Movement by a player in control of the ball (within playing distance) designed to prevent an opponent from gaining possession or tackling the ball. This is a legal maneuver.

sliding tackle—A maneuver in which one or both feet slide on the ground in trying to tackle the ball that is in the possession of an opponent.

substitute—A team member who has properly reported to enter the game. A substitute becomes a player when he or she is beckoned onto the field of play by an official.

suspended—A term indicating that a game has been interrupted by the referee because of conditions that make it impossible to continue play; these conditions are not the fault of the participants or spectators. Examples of such conditions include inclement weather, power failure or any other emergency affecting playing conditions.

tackle—The use of the feet to take a ball away from a player in control of the ball.

taunting—The use of words or actions to incite or degrade an opposing player, coach, referee or other people at the game.

terminated—A term that indicates that a game has been ended by the referee for action of the participants or spectators, such as refusal to play or disorder. The status of the game, which might include forfeiture, will be determined by the proper authority.

throw-in—A method by which a dead ball becomes alive. A player throws the ball using both hands. The ball must be delivered from behind and over the head in one continuous movement, while both feet are on the ground and on or behind the touchline. The player must be facing the field.

touchlines—These are the longer, or side, boundary lines. The entire line is within the field of play.

violent conduct—The commission of a violent act against an opponent, an official, a spectator, a teammate or other individuals when the ball is in or out of play.

warning—A verbal admonition to a coach or player for conduct not in the best interest of the game. Repeat warnings necessitate an official caution.

INDEX

Note: The italicized *f* following page numbers refers to figures.

ABOUT THE AUTHOR

Officiating Soccer was written by the American Sport Education Program (ASEP) in cooperation with the National Federation of State High School Associations (NFHS). Based in Indianapolis, the NFHS is the rules authority for high school sports in the United States. Hundreds of thousands of officials nationwide and throughout the world rely on the NFHS for officiating guidance. ASEP is a division of Human Kinetics, based in Champaign, Illinois, and has been a world leader in providing educational courses and resources to professional and volunteer coaches, officials, parents, and sport administrators for more than 20 years. ASEP and NFHS have teamed up to offer courses for high school officials through the NFHS Officials Education Program.

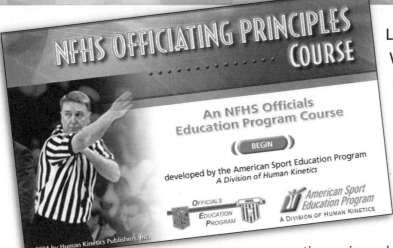